MONTREUX

TRAVEL GUIDE 2024

DISCOVER THE BEAUTY, CULTURE AND ADVENTURE OF MONTREUX

ANITA PHIPPS

Copyright © 2024

All rights reserved. No part of this book may be reproduced, distributed, or transmitted in any form or by any means, including photocopying, recording, or other electronic or mechanical methods, without the prior written permission of the owner.except in the case of brief quotations embodied in critical reviews and certain other noncommercial uses permitted by copyright law.

- Introduction to Montreux
  - Overview of Montreux
  - History and Culture
  - Geography and Climate
- Planning Your Trip
  - Best Time to Visit Montreux
  - Getting Around Montreux
  - Visa and Entry Requirements
- Accommodation Options
  - Hotels
  - Bed and Breakfasts
  - Vacation Rentals
- Attractions and Landmarks
  - Château de Chillon
  - Montreux Lakeside Promenade
  - Freddie Mercury Statue
  - Montreux Jazz Festival
  - Rochers-de-Naye
  - Vevey (nearby town)
  - Lavaux Vineyards (UNESCO World Heritage Site)
- Outdoor Activities
  - Hiking and Trekking in the Alps
  - Lake Geneva Boat Cruises
  - Cycling Routes
  - Water Sports (Kayaking, Stand-Up Paddleboarding)
  - Skiing and Snowboarding (winter season)
- Dining and Cuisine
  - Swiss Cuisine and Specialty Dishes
  - Fondue and Raclette Restaurants
  - Lakeside Dining
  - Local Markets and Food Festivals
- Shopping
  - Swiss Watches and Chocolate
  - Souvenirs and Gifts
  - Boutique Shops and Artisanal Crafts
- Nightlife and Entertainment
  - Bars and Pubs
  - Live Music Venues
  - Casino Barrière de Montreux

Wellness and relaxation
    Spa Resorts and Wellness Centers
    Thermal Baths
    Yoga and Meditation Classes
    Lakeside Relaxation Spots
Day Trips from Montreux
    Lausanne
    Gruyères
    Glacier 3000
    Montreux Riviera Cruise
Practical Tips and Advice
    Safety Tips
    Budgeting and Money Matters
    Local Customs and Etiquette
    Sustainable Travel Practices
Conclusion and Additional Resources
    Useful Websites and Apps
    Acknowledgment
    Maps

Introduction to Montreux

Overview of Montreux

Nestled along the eastern shores of Lake Geneva in Switzerland, Montreux is a town that oozes charm and sophistication. Its stunning natural setting, nestled between the majestic Alps and the sparkling lake, has captivated travelers for centuries. From its Belle Époque grandeur to its vibrant cultural scene, Montreux offers a unique blend of experiences that cater to all types of travelers.

A Rich History Steeped in Culture

The town boasts a rich history dating back to the 12th century. The iconic Château de Chillon, perched on a rocky outcrop overlooking the lake, is a testament to its medieval past. Montreux also played a significant role in the development of tourism in the 19th century, attracting wealthy travelers from across Europe with its mild climate and luxurious hotels.

A Celebration of Music and the Arts

Today, Montreux is renowned for its vibrant cultural scene. The world-famous Montreux Jazz Festival, held every summer, attracts legendary musicians and music lovers alike. The town also hosts numerous other festivals throughout the year, celebrating everything from classical music and film to flowers and Christmas markets.

Beyond the Festival Scene

But there's more to Montreux than just festivals. The charming lakeside promenade lined with Belle Époque hotels and cafes invites leisurely strolls. You can also explore the charming medieval old town, with its narrow streets and traditional shops.

A Paradise for Outdoor Enthusiasts

For those seeking outdoor adventure, Montreux is surrounded by breathtaking scenery. Hike or bike through the vineyards of Lavaux, a UNESCO World Heritage Site, or take a cable car ride up to the Rochers-de-Naye for panoramic views of the lake and the Alps.

A Foodie's Delight

Montreux is a haven for food lovers. Sample traditional Swiss dishes like fondue and raclette, or indulge in fresh seafood and local delicacies. The town also boasts a diverse selection of restaurants, from Michelin-starred establishments to cozy cafes.

A Perfect Escape for All Seasons

Whether you're seeking a romantic getaway, a cultural immersion, or an outdoor adventure, Montreux has something to offer everyone. With its stunning scenery, rich history, vibrant culture, and delicious food, this charming Swiss town is sure to leave you with unforgettable memories.

Here are some additional things to keep in mind when planning your trip to Montreux:

- The best time to visit Montreux is during the spring and summer months, when the weather is mild and sunny. However, the town also has a festive charm during the winter holidays.
- Montreux is a relatively small town, so it's easy to get around on foot or by bike. However, there is also a public transportation system that includes buses and trains.
- The official language of Montreux is French, but English is widely spoken.
- The currency in Switzerland is the Swiss franc (CHF).

History and Culture

Montreux isn't just a town; it's a living tapestry twisted with centuries of history and vibrant culture. Step off the train and into a world where medieval fortresses whisper tales of knights and damsels, Belle Époque elegance mingles with modern sophistication, and music fills the air like a sweet perfume.

Medieval Marvels:

Wander the imposing halls of **Château de Chillon**, a stone sentinel guarding the lake for over a thousand years. Imagine knights clashing swords in its courtyards, or prisoners yearning for freedom in its damp dungeons. The very stones whisper stories of intrigue and adventure.

Belle Époque Boom:

Fast forward to the 19th century, and Montreux transforms into a playground for the rich and famous. Step into the opulent **Fairmont Le Montreux Palace**, its ornate balconies echoing with laughter from bygone balls. Imagine Charlie Chaplin strolling along the promenade, or Audrey Hepburn sipping tea on a lakeside terrace.

Music Makes the Magic:

But Montreux truly comes alive with music. The legendary **Montreux Jazz Festival** draws music lovers from around the globe, its stages pulsating with the sounds of legendary artists and rising stars. Imagine swaying to the soulful melodies of Nina Simone or the electrifying riffs of Deep Purple. Music doesn't just fill the air; it becomes a shared experience, a joyous celebration.

Beyond the Festival:

Delve deeper and discover the soul of Montreux. Explore the charming **old town**, its cobbled streets lined with colorful houses and quaint cafes. Chat with friendly locals over steaming mugs of coffee, and hear stories passed down through generations. Immerse yourself in the festive spirit of the **Christmas markets**, with their twinkling lights and irresistible aromas.

Traditions Alive:

Witness the vibrant **Fête des Vignerons**, a centuries-old wine festival that celebrates the region's rich viticultural heritage. Watch as elaborately costumed figures parade through the streets, their laughter and music echoing a deep connection to the land.

Modern Innovation:

Montreux isn't stuck in the past. Visit the **Câbrol House**, once Charlie Chaplin's final residence, now a museum dedicated to his silent film genius. Or peek into the future at the **Swiss Federal Institute of Technology**, where cutting-edge research pushes the boundaries of innovation.

Your Story Awaits:

Montreux isn't just a place to visit; it's a place to feel, to experience, to create your own story. So, pack your bags, embrace the magic, and let history, culture, and music draw you into the captivating world of Montreux!

Geography and Climate

This city isn't just a town rich in history and culture; it's also a stunning example of breathtaking geography and a delightfully mild climate. Buckle up as we explore the natural beauty and charming weather that make Montreux a truly unique destination.

A Lakeside Paradise:

Imagine this: crystal-clear waters of Lake Geneva shimmering under the sun, reflecting the snow-capped peaks of the Swiss Alps that rise majestically in the distance. This is the picture-perfect setting of Montreux, where you can stroll along the lakefront promenade, soaking in the fresh air and the panoramic views. Whether you're taking a romantic boat ride or simply enjoying a picnic by the water, the lake becomes an integral part of the Montreux experience.

Mountains that Inspire:

But Montreux isn't just about the water; it's also about the majestic mountains that cradle the town. Hike or bike through the lush vineyards of Lavaux, a UNESCO World Heritage Site, and marvel at the patchwork of emerald vines cascading down the slopes. Take a cable car ride up to the Rochers-de-Naye and be awestruck by the breathtaking panorama of the lake and the Alps stretching out before you. In winter, these slopes transform into a skier's paradise, offering unforgettable adventures for snow enthusiasts.

A Climate for All Seasons:

Unlike other alpine towns, Montreux boasts a surprisingly mild climate thanks to its sheltered location on the lake. Spring and summer bring warm sunshine, perfect for exploring the outdoors and enjoying the lakefront activities. Autumn paints the landscapes in fiery hues, and winter offers a magical snowy wonderland. Even during the coldest months, the temperatures rarely drop below freezing, making Montreux a year-round destination.

Nature's Playground:

Whether you're seeking gentle walks along the lake or challenging hikes in the mountains, Montreux has something for everyone. Explore the gorges and waterfalls hidden within the valleys, or cycle through charming villages nestled amongst the vineyards. The fresh mountain air and the diverse landscapes will invigorate your senses and leave you feeling refreshed and rejuvenated.

Beyond the Scenery:

Montreux's geographical location has also played a significant role in its cultural development. The mild climate attracted artists and celebrities in the 19th century, and the surrounding mountains provided inspiration for countless writers and musicians. This unique blend of nature and culture continues to shape Montreux's identity today.

So, whether you're a nature enthusiast seeking breathtaking scenery or a traveler drawn to cultural richness, Montreux offers a unique blend of geography and climate that will leave you wanting more. Pack your bags, breathe in the fresh air, and immerse yourself in the natural beauty that awaits you in this enchanting Swiss town.

Planning Your Trip

Best Time to Visit Montreux

Finding your perfect Montreux moment:

Montreux's diverse landscape and vibrant cultural scene offer something for everyone, year-round. But to truly optimize your experience, consider the unique charm of each season:

Spring (March-May):

- **Pros:** Pleasant temperatures, blooming flowers, fewer crowds, and lower prices compared to peak season.
- **Cons:** Some outdoor activities and boat tours might not be operational yet.

- **Highlights:** Witness the narcissus bloom in the surrounding hills, enjoy mild weather for outdoor exploration, and experience the Easter celebrations with traditional processions and markets.

Summer (June-August):

- **Pros:** Warmest weather, ideal for swimming in the lake, vibrant festivals like the Montreux Jazz Festival, and longer daylight hours.
- **Cons:** Peak tourist season, meaning higher prices and larger crowds.
- **Highlights:** Immerse yourself in the world-famous Jazz Festival, bask on the lakeside beaches, take a boat cruise on Lake Geneva, and enjoy outdoor activities like hiking and biking.

Autumn (September-November):

- **Pros:** Comfortable temperatures, colorful fall foliage, fewer crowds compared to summer, and grape harvest festivals in the surrounding Lavaux vineyards.
- **Cons:** Some outdoor activities and boat tours might have limited schedules.
- **Highlights:** Hike through the vineyards adorned in fiery hues, savor local delicacies during grape harvest festivals, and experience the Christmas markets starting in late November.

Winter (December-February):

- **Pros:** Magical Christmas markets, festive atmosphere, winter sports opportunities in nearby resorts, and potentially lower prices compared to peak season.
- **Cons:** Colder temperatures, shorter daylight hours, and some outdoor activities might be unavailable.

- **Highlights:** Immerse yourself in the enchanting Christmas markets, enjoy winter sports like skiing and snowboarding in the surrounding mountains, and witness the New Year's Eve celebrations on the lakeside promenade.

Ultimately, the best time to visit Montreux depends on your personal preferences and priorities. Consider what kind of weather you enjoy, what activities you're interested in, and the budget you have in mind.

Additional tips:

- If you're on a tight budget, consider visiting during the shoulder seasons (spring or autumn) when prices are generally lower.
- If you're specifically interested in attending a particular festival or event, plan your trip accordingly.
- Be sure to book your accommodation and activities in advance, especially during peak season.

Getting Around Montreux

Lodge between glistening waters and snow-capped peaks, a captivating town awaits. But when should you embark on your journey? Let's explore the unique charm of each season:

Spring (March-May):

- **Blossoming beauty:** Witness vibrant blooms paint the landscape, with pleasant temperatures perfect for exploration.
- **Fewer crowds, lower costs:** Enjoy budget-friendly escapes and explore without the summer rush.
- **Easter festivities:** Immerse yourself in traditional processions and vibrant markets celebrating the season.

Summer (June-August):

- **Warmest embrace:** Bask in the sun, swim in the serene lake, and experience longer days for adventure.
- **Festival fever:** Immerse yourself in the world-famous Jazz Festival and other vibrant events.
- **Outdoor paradise:** Hike, bike, and boat your way through breathtaking landscapes.

Autumn (September-November):

- **Fiery hues:** Witness vineyards transform into a tapestry of fiery colors, perfect for scenic hikes.
- **Grape harvest bounty:** Savor local delicacies and celebrate the harvest with charming festivals.
- **Christmas markets begin:** Get a taste of the festive spirit with early markets and twinkling lights.

Winter (December-February):

- **Magical wonderland:** Soak in the festive atmosphere with enchanting Christmas markets.
- **Winter sports haven:** Hit the slopes in nearby resorts for exhilarating adventures.
- **Lower costs:** Enjoy potentially lower prices compared to peak season.

Finding Your Ideal Path:

Reaching this charming haven offers various options, each with its own advantages:

Soaring Through the Clouds:

- **Closest companion:** Geneva International Airport, conveniently located just a stone's throw away.

- **Multiple connections:** Numerous airlines offer direct and connecting flights from major cities worldwide.
- **Swiftest option:** Perfect for time-conscious travelers, especially from faraway lands.

Embracing the Rails:

- **Seamless network:** Connect to major Swiss, French, and European cities with ease.
- **Scenic journey:** Relax and enjoy the breathtaking Alpine vistas as you travel.
- **Consideration:** Train tickets can be costly, especially for long distances.

Hitting the Road:

- **Flexibility and freedom:** Explore at your own pace and discover hidden gems along the way.
- **Scenic drives:** Enjoy the beauty of the Alps as you navigate well-maintained roads.
- **Cost considerations:** Tolls and parking can add to the expense.

Budget-Friendly Rides:

- **Bus connections:** Reach your destination comfortably at a more affordable price.
- **Longer travel times:** Be prepared for longer journeys compared to other options.

Remember, the perfect time and mode of travel depend on your preferences and priorities. Consider the weather, activities you desire, and budget constraints to make the ideal choice.

Visa and Entry Requirements

General Information:

here's a general overview of visa and entry requirements for Switzerland:

- **Schengen Visa:** Most visitors from countries outside the European Union (EU) and Schengen Area require a Schengen visa to enter Switzerland. This visa allows you to stay in the Schengen Area for up to 90 days within a 180-day period.
- **Visa-free Travel:** Citizens of certain countries can visit Switzerland visa-free for short stays. Check if your country is on the list of visa-exempt countries on the official Swiss government website.
- **Entry Requirements:** Even if you don't need a visa, you may still need to meet other entry requirements, such as having a valid passport with sufficient blank pages, proof of travel insurance, and sufficient funds for your stay.

Additional Resources:

For the most up-to-date and accurate information, it's recommended to consult the official Swiss government website or contact the nearest Swiss embassy or consulate in your home country.

Accommodation Options

Hotels

Now that you've conquered the visa hurdles, let's explore the world of hotels in the charming town you're yearning to visit. Remember, I can't mention the specific town name, but I can offer a diverse range of options based on your preferences and budget.

Luxury Indulgence:

- **Fairmont Le Montreux Palace (Lakeside):** Immerse yourself in unparalleled luxury at this iconic palace. Opulent rooms, a Michelin-starred restaurant, and a world-renowned jazz festival held within its walls await. Unwind in the Willow Stream Spa or take a dip in the heated outdoor pool, all while soaking in breathtaking lake views.
- **Grand Hotel Suisse Majestic (Lakeside):** Step back in time to Belle Époque grandeur. Elegant rooms with panoramic lake views, a rooftop terrace with stunning vistas, and a renowned restaurant serving exquisite Swiss cuisine offer a truly unforgettable experience.

Boutique Charm:

- **Hotel de la Paix (Central):** Experience Swiss hospitality at its finest. Personalized service, comfortable rooms with traditional décor, and a central location close to shops, restaurants, and the lakeside promenade make this a delightful choice.
- **Hôtel Byron (Quiet Residential Area):** Nestled away from the hustle and bustle, this charming hotel offers a peaceful retreat. Cozy rooms with balconies, a beautiful garden for relaxation, and a delightful breakfast terrace set the scene for a tranquil stay.

Budget-Friendly Stays:

- **Auberge de Jeunesse Montreux (Central):** Enjoy a social and affordable stay at this centrally located youth hostel. Comfortable dorm rooms, a communal kitchen, a lively atmosphere, and proximity to public transport make it a great option for budget-conscious travelers.
- **Hôtel du Parc et Lac (Near Lake and Train Station):** This family-run hotel provides a welcoming and budget-friendly option. Simple

yet comfortable rooms, a pizzeria on-site, and a convenient location near the lake and train station make it a practical and comfortable choice.

Unique Experiences:

- **BnB Les Nénuphars (Lakefront):** Stay in a charming Swiss chalet with stunning lake views. This bed and breakfast offers a unique and personalized experience, with comfortable rooms, a communal living area with a fireplace, and a delicious breakfast served on the terrace overlooking the lake.
- **Camping Les Grangettes (Lakefront):** Pitch your tent or rent a cabin right on the lakeside at this campsite. Perfect for nature lovers seeking an authentic and affordable adventure, the campsite offers basic amenities like showers, laundry facilities, and a snack bar.

Remember:

- **Consider your budget:** Hotels in Switzerland can range from luxury palaces to budget-friendly hostels. Choose the option that best suits your spending preferences.
- **Location:** Do you want to be in the heart of the action or prefer a quieter location? Consider proximity to attractions, public transport, and amenities.
- **Amenities:** What amenities are important to you, such as a spa, fitness center, swimming pool, balcony, or lake views?
- **Read reviews:** Check online reviews to get a sense of other guests' experiences before booking.

By considering these factors and exploring the diverse range of hotels available, you're sure to find the perfect nest for your unforgettable escape!

Bed and Breakfasts

Here's a revamped list of captivating Bed and Breakfasts in the charming town you're yearning to visit, complete with locations and amenities:

Embrace the Intimacy of Bed and Breakfasts:

If you seek a more personal and homey experience, consider these delightful Bed and Breakfasts:

- **BnB Les Nénuphars (Lakefront):** Immerse yourself in the charm of a traditional Swiss chalet with stunning lake views. This B&B offers a unique and personalized experience, with comfortable rooms, a communal living area with a fireplace, and a delicious breakfast served on the terrace overlooking the lake.
- **Marché 28 Guesthouse (Central):** Situated in a historic building close to the lakeside promenade and the marketplace, this B&B boasts cozy rooms with balconies, a shared kitchen, and a charming garden. Enjoy a continental breakfast served in the communal dining room.
- **Room next Montreux (Central):** This modern B&B offers stylish rooms with balconies or terraces, a shared kitchen, and a comfortable lounge area. Start your day with a delicious breakfast buffet served in the bright and airy dining room.
- **La plus belle vue du lac Léman (Near Lake):** As the name suggests, this B&B boasts breathtaking views of Lake Geneva. Relax in comfortable rooms with balconies, enjoy a shared lounge with a fireplace, and savor a homemade breakfast on the terrace while soaking up the scenery.
- **Chambre double vue lac Montreux center (Central):** Located in the heart of town, this B&B offers a double room with a stunning lake view, a balcony, and access to a shared kitchen and living area. Enjoy a continental breakfast served in your room or on the balcony.

Additional Tips:

- **Consider your budget:** B&Bs generally offer more affordable rates compared to hotels, but prices can vary depending on location, amenities, and season.
- **Amenities:** Some B&Bs offer shared kitchens, laundry facilities, and gardens, while others provide more limited amenities. Choose a B&B that offers the amenities you value most.
- **Breakfast:** Most B&Bs include breakfast in their rates, offering a chance to sample local flavors and interact with your hosts.
- **Personal touch:** B&Bs often provide a more personalized experience than hotels, with hosts who can offer recommendations and local insights.

By considering these factors and exploring the diverse range of B&Bs available, you're sure to find the perfect home away from home for your charming Swiss escape!

Vacation Rentals

Here's a curated selection of vacation rentals in this captivating town you're yearning to visit, complete with locations and details that might entice you:

Immerse Yourself in the Local Charm:

For a truly immersive experience, consider vacation rentals that offer a taste of local life and the freedom of a home away from home:

- **Charming Studio with Balcony and Lake View (Central):** Nestled in the heart of town, this modern studio apartment boasts a private balcony with breathtaking lake views. Enjoy a fully equipped kitchen, a cozy living area, and a comfortable sleeping space. Perfect for couples or solo travelers seeking a central location and stunning scenery.

- **Spacious Apartment with Terrace and Panoramic Views (Near Lake):** This spacious apartment offers stunning panoramic views of the lake and mountains. Relax on the expansive terrace, cook up a feast in the fully equipped kitchen, and gather with loved ones in the comfortable living area. Ideal for families or groups seeking a homey atmosphere and breathtaking vistas.
- **Cozy Cottage with Garden and Fireplace (Quiet Residential Area):** Escape the hustle and bustle in this charming cottage located in a quiet residential neighborhood. Relax by the fireplace, cook up meals in the fully equipped kitchen, and enjoy the tranquility of the private garden. Perfect for nature lovers and those seeking a peaceful retreat.
- **Lakeside Villa with Private Pool and Jacuzzi (Lakefront):** Indulge in ultimate luxury at this stunning villa nestled directly on the lakefront. Featuring a private pool, jacuzzi, spacious bedrooms, a fully equipped kitchen, and multiple terraces with breathtaking views, this villa is perfect for groups or families seeking an unforgettable lakeside experience.
- **Historic Chalet with Sauna and Mountain Views (Mountainside):** Immerse yourself in the charm of a traditional Swiss chalet with breathtaking mountain views. Relax in the sauna after a day of exploring, gather around the fireplace in the evenings, and enjoy the tranquility of the mountainside location. This chalet is perfect for groups or families seeking a unique and authentic Swiss experience.

Additional Tips:

- **Consider your budget:** Vacation rentals can range in price depending on location, size, amenities, and season. Choose a rental that fits your budget and needs.

- **Amenities:** Some rentals offer amenities like private balconies, pools, gardens, fireplaces, and saunas. Choose a rental that offers the amenities you value most.
- **Location:** Do you want to be in the heart of town or prefer a quieter location? Consider proximity to attractions, public transport, and amenities.
- **Reviews:** Read reviews from other guests to get a sense of the rental's condition, amenities, and host responsiveness.

By considering these factors and exploring the diverse range of vacation rentals available, you're sure to find the perfect home away from home for your captivating Swiss escape!

Attractions and Landmarks

Château de Chillon

often referred to as the "Castle of Chillon," is a magnificent medieval fortress situated on a rocky islet in Lake Geneva, near the town of Veytaux, Switzerland. Here's what you need to know about this captivating landmark:

A Journey Through Time:

Dating back to the 12th century, the castle has served as a strategic military stronghold, a noble residence, and even a prison throughout its rich history. Its imposing walls and towers have witnessed centuries of significant events and are now a popular tourist destination, attracting visitors from around the globe.

Exploring the Castle:

A visit to Château de Chillon allows you to step back in time and explore its various chambers, halls, and courtyards. Here are some highlights:

- **The Great Hall:** This impressive hall once served as the main gathering place for the castle's residents. Its high ceilings, stone pillars, and grand fireplaces create a sense of grandeur and history.
- **The Ducal Apartments:** Once home to the castle's noble residents, these apartments offer a glimpse into their luxurious lifestyle. Tapestries, furniture, and other artifacts showcase the opulence of the era.
- **The Subterranean Chambers:** Delve into the castle's darker side by exploring the dungeons and torture chambers. These dimly lit spaces offer a chilling reminder of the castle's past as a prison.
- **The Camera Obscura:** This unique optical device projects an inverted image of the surrounding landscape onto a screen. It's a fascinating way to experience the views from the castle in a different perspective.

Beyond the Walls:

Besides exploring the castle itself, you can also:

- **Wander the charming village of Veytaux:** Located at the foot of the castle, this picturesque village offers stunning lake views and a variety of restaurants and shops.
- **Take a boat tour on Lake Geneva:** Enjoy breathtaking views of the castle and the surrounding mountains from the water.
- **Hike or bike in the surrounding vineyards:** The area around the castle is known for its beautiful scenery and offers plenty of opportunities for outdoor activities.

Planning Your Visit:

- The castle is open year-round, with extended hours during the summer season.
- Tickets can be purchased online or at the entrance.

- Guided tours are available in various languages.
- Consider purchasing a Swiss Travel Pass for discounted travel on public transport, including ferries and trains to reach the castle.

With its rich history, captivating architecture, and stunning setting, Château de Chillon is a must-visit for anyone exploring Switzerland.

Montreux Lakeside Promenade

The Montreux Lakeside Promenade is a captivating walkway that stretches for nearly seven kilometers along the shores of Lake Geneva, offering breathtaking scenery, vibrant atmosphere, and countless things to discover. Here's a detailed look:

A Scenic Stroll by the Lake:

Imagine strolling along a picturesque path flanked by lush greenery, sparkling lake waters, and snow-capped mountains in the distance. This is the quintessential experience that awaits you on the Montreux Lakeside Promenade. This car-free walkway is the heart of the town, bustling with life throughout the year.

Highlights Along the Promenade:

- **Stunning Panoramic Views:** As you walk along the promenade, you'll be mesmerized by the ever-changing vistas of Lake Geneva and the majestic Alps. The interplay of light and colors creates a breathtaking backdrop for your stroll.
- **Vibrant Atmosphere:** The promenade is a melting pot of locals and tourists, enjoying the fresh air, engaging in street performances, and soaking in the lively atmosphere. From musicians and artists to vendors selling local crafts and souvenirs, there's always something to see and do.

- **Historical Landmarks:** Dotted along the promenade are several historical landmarks that tell the story of Montreux. The iconic Château de Chillon stands proudly on a rocky islet, while the Belle Époque architecture of the Fairmont Le Montreux Palace adds a touch of grandeur. Don't miss the Freddie Mercury statue, a tribute to the legendary Queen frontman who spent his final years in Montreux.
- **Relaxation and Recreation:** Whether you're seeking a leisurely stroll, a bike ride, or a picnic by the lake, the promenade caters to all preferences. Relax on one of the many benches, enjoy a refreshing gelato, or rent a paddleboat and explore the lake from a different perspective.
- **Cultural Experiences:** Throughout the year, the promenade comes alive with various cultural events and festivals. Immerse yourself in the vibrant atmosphere of the Montreux Jazz Festival, savor local delicacies at the Christmas markets, or witness the dazzling spectacle of the Montreux Christmas Parade.

Beyond the Promenade:

While the promenade itself offers endless enjoyment, venturing beyond its path opens doors to further exploration:

- **Charming Town Center:** Explore the charming streets of Montreux, lined with boutiques, cafes, and restaurants. Immerse yourself in the local culture and discover hidden gems.
- **Vineyards of Lavaux:** The UNESCO World Heritage Site of Lavaux, with its cascading vineyards and picturesque villages, is easily accessible from the promenade. Hike or bike through the vineyards, visit local wineries, and savor the region's delicious wines.

- **Lakeside Activities:** From boat cruises and paddleboarding to swimming and stand-up paddleboarding, Lake Geneva offers a variety of activities for water enthusiasts.

Planning Your Visit:

- The promenade is open year-round and accessible free of charge.
- Wear comfortable shoes suitable for walking.
- Pack sunscreen and a hat, especially during the summer months.
- Consider purchasing the Swiss Travel Pass for discounted travel on public transport, including trains to reach Montreux.

With its stunning scenery, vibrant atmosphere, and diverse offerings, the Montreux Lakeside Promenade is a must-visit for anyone exploring Switzerland. So lace up your walking shoes, breathe in the fresh air, and prepare to be captivated by the magic of this charming lakeside path!

Freddie Mercury Statue

Standing tall on the Montreux Lakeside Promenade, the Freddie Mercury statue is a powerful and poignant tribute to the legendary Queen frontman. More than just a tourist attraction, it's a symbol of Freddie's love for the town and the enduring legacy of his music.

Capturing Freddie's Essence:

Sculpted by Irena Sedlecká, the statue portrays Freddie in a dynamic pose, arms outstretched, microphone stand in hand, belting out a song. The bronze figure, nearly three meters tall, captures Freddie's larger-than-life stage presence and infectious energy.

A Symbol of Love and Connection:

The statue was unveiled in 1996, five years after Freddie's passing. It has since become a beloved landmark, visited by fans from all over the world. Visitors often leave flowers, messages, and tributes around the statue, creating a tangible connection to Freddie's memory.

Beyond the Memorial:

The statue is more than just a static memorial. It serves as a reminder of Freddie's deep connection to Montreux. He lived and recorded music in the town for years, finding solace and inspiration in its beauty. The statue embodies this connection, making it a cherished landmark for both fans and locals.

A Lasting Legacy:

The Freddie Mercury statue serves as a powerful reminder of the enduring legacy of Freddie's music and his impact on the world. It's a testament to his talent, his passion, and his ability to connect with people through his music. As long as his music continues to inspire and move people, Freddie's spirit will live on in this iconic statue and in the hearts of his fans.

Planning Your Visit:

- The statue is located on the Montreux Lakeside Promenade, near the Casino Barrière de Montreux.
- It is accessible free of charge and open to the public 24/7.
- Consider visiting during the Freddie Celebration Days in Montreux, held annually in September, to immerse yourself in the town's celebration of Freddie's legacy.

Whether you're a dedicated Queen fan or simply appreciate artistic expression, the Freddie Mercury statue in Montreux is a must-see for anyone visiting the town. It's a powerful symbol of music, love, and the enduring legacy of a true legend.

Montreux Jazz Festival

Taking place every summer for two weeks in July, the Montreux Jazz Festival is a world-renowned event that attracts music lovers from all corners of the globe. Held on the shores of the picturesque Lake Geneva in Switzerland, the festival offers a unique blend of musical genres, stunning scenery, and a vibrant atmosphere.

A Rich History:

Founded in 1967 by Claude Nobs, the festival started as a small jazz event. However, over the years, it has evolved into a major international music festival, showcasing a diverse range of genres from jazz and blues to rock, pop, and electronic music.

Legendary Performances:

The Montreux Jazz Festival has seen some of the biggest names in music grace its stages, including Miles Davis, Nina Simone, Marvin Gaye, B.B. King, David Bowie, Stevie Wonder, Radiohead, and Beyoncé.

More Than Just Music:

Apart from the main concerts, the festival also features a variety of other events and activities, such as free open-air concerts, workshops, film screenings, and art exhibitions. This creates a truly immersive experience for festival attendees.

Unique Festival Atmosphere:

With its stunning lakeside setting, vibrant atmosphere, and diverse musical offerings, the Montreux Jazz Festival is an unforgettable experience. It's a place where music lovers can come together to celebrate their passion and discover new sounds.

Planning Your Visit:

- **Dates:** The Montreux Jazz Festival typically takes place in July.
- **Tickets:** Tickets can be purchased online or at the festival box office.
- **Accommodation:** Book your accommodation well in advance, as the festival attracts a large number of visitors.
- **Transportation:** The Montreux Jazz Festival is easily accessible by train, bus, or car.

Additional Tips:

- Pack for all types of weather, as the Swiss summer can be unpredictable.
- Wear comfortable shoes, as you'll be doing a lot of walking.
- Bring a reusable water bottle to stay hydrated.
- Don't forget your sunscreen and hat.
- Be prepared for crowds, especially during the headliner concerts.

Rochers-de-Naye

The Rochers-de-Naye is a mountain peak in the Swiss Alps, overlooking Lake Geneva near Montreux and Villeneuve, in the canton of Vaud. With its peak reaching 2,042 meters (6,699 feet), it offers breathtaking panoramic views of the surrounding mountains and valleys, making it a popular destination for tourists and nature enthusiasts alike.

Reaching the Summit:

Reaching the summit of the Rochers-de-Naye is an experience in itself. You can take the Montreux–Glion–Rochers-de-Naye railway, which is the highest railway in the canton of Vaud and offers stunning views along the way. The journey takes about 35 minutes, climbing more than 1,600 meters (5,250 feet) in altitude.

Activities and Attractions:

Once you reach the summit, you can enjoy a variety of activities and attractions, including:

- **Panoramic views:** Take in the breathtaking 360-degree views of Lake Geneva, the Swiss Alps, and the Jura mountains.
- **Alpine Garden La Rambertia:** Explore this unique botanical garden, home to over 1,000 species of alpine plants from around the world.
- **Marmot Paradise:** Observe these adorable alpine rodents in their natural habitat.
- **Playground:** Let the kids have fun in a large playground with slides, swings, and climbing structures.
- **Restaurants:** Enjoy a delicious meal at one of the restaurants at the summit, offering panoramic views and local specialties.

Seasonal Activities:

Depending on the season, you can also enjoy a variety of seasonal activities at the Rochers-de-Naye, such as:

- **Winter sports:** In winter, the Rochers-de-Naye becomes a popular ski resort, offering stunning views and challenging slopes.
- **Hiking and biking:** In summer, you can enjoy hiking and biking trails with breathtaking views.

- **Snowshoeing and cross-country skiing:** In winter, you can enjoy snowshoeing and cross-country skiing trails through the beautiful snowy landscape.

Planning Your Visit:

- The Rochers-de-Naye is open year-round, but the opening hours vary depending on the season.
- Tickets for the train and the summit can be purchased online or at the station.
- Be sure to dress warmly, as the weather at the summit can be much colder than in the valley.
- Wear comfortable shoes, as there is a lot of walking involved.

Vevey (nearby town)

Vevey, the charming town nestled on the shores of Lake Geneva, is a vibrant gem waiting to be explored. Here's a glimpse into what awaits you in this captivating Swiss destination:

A Historical Tapestry:

Vevey boasts a rich history dating back to Roman times, evident in its architectural treasures. Stroll through the charming Old Town, where cobbled streets wind past medieval houses, quaint shops, and historical landmarks like the 12th-century Vevey Castle.

Immerse yourself in the town's cultural heritage at the Jenisch Museum, showcasing an impressive collection of art and artifacts. Don't miss the Musée Chaplin, dedicated to the legendary Charlie Chaplin who spent his final years here, offering a glimpse into his life and work.

A Foodie Paradise:

Vevey is a haven for food lovers, known as the birthplace of Nestlé and home to the Alimentarium, a unique food museum exploring culinary history and traditions. Savor local delicacies at charming cafes and restaurants, or browse the vibrant market for fresh produce and regional specialties.

Lakeside Enchantment:

The crown jewel of Vevey is undoubtedly its stunning lakeside promenade. Embark on a leisurely stroll or bike ride, soaking in the breathtaking views of Lake Geneva and the majestic Alps. During summer, the promenade comes alive with vibrant flower displays, street performers, and buzzing cafes.

Year-Round Festivities:

Vevey's cultural calendar is brimming with exciting events throughout the year. Immerse yourself in the festive spirit of the Images Festival, celebrating photography and visual arts, or witness the dazzling spectacle of the Christmas markets. Don't miss the world-renowned Montreux Jazz Festival, held nearby, for an unforgettable musical experience.

Beyond the Town:

Vevey is an ideal base for exploring the surrounding region. Take a scenic boat trip across Lake Geneva, visit the charming vineyards of Lavaux, or embark on a thrilling hike in the nearby mountains.

Planning Your Visit:

- **Getting there:** Vevey is easily accessible by train or car from major Swiss cities like Geneva and Lausanne.
- **Accommodation:** The town offers a range of accommodation options, from charming boutique hotels to modern apartments.
- **Currency:** Switzerland uses the Swiss Franc (CHF).

- **Language:** French is the primary language spoken in Vevey, but English is widely understood.

With its rich history, vibrant culture, stunning scenery, and delicious food, Vevey promises a truly unforgettable experience. So pack your bags and embark on your own Swiss adventure!

Lavaux Vineyards (UNESCO World Heritage Site)

The Lavaux Vineyards, a UNESCO World Heritage Site, are like a dream come true for any wine lover or nature enthusiast. Imagine rolling hills, lush greenery, and meticulously sculpted terraces cascading down to the shores of Lake Geneva. This breathtaking landscape, nestled between Lausanne and Montreux, is a tapestry of beauty, history, and of course, delicious wines.

The story of these vineyards goes way back, over 1,000 years in fact! Benedictine and Cistercian monks played a big role in shaping the landscape, building those impressive stone walls that not only prevent erosion but also help the grapes get the most sunshine. It's pretty cool how these walls have been meticulously maintained for centuries, creating a unique microclimate that contributes to the region's special wines.

Wandering through the Lavaux vineyards is like stepping into a painting. The terraced slopes adorned with rows of grapevines create a mesmerizing patchwork against the backdrop of the majestic Alps and the shimmering lake. Each season brings a new touch of magic, from the vibrant greens of spring to the golden hues of autumn.

But Lavaux isn't just about the views (although they are pretty incredible). Winemaking is deeply ingrained in the region's culture. You'll find charming family-run wineries nestled amidst the vineyards, where generations of winemakers have perfected their craft. Be sure to sample some of the local wines, from crisp Chasselas whites to full-bodied Pinot Noirs, each reflecting the unique character of the land and the dedication of the people who make them. And don't forget to pair your wine with some local cheese, charcuterie, and fresh bread – pure deliciousness!

The vineyards offer more than just wine and stunning scenery. Lace up your hiking boots and explore the numerous trails that crisscross the region, or cycle along the scenic roads, taking in the fresh air and breathtaking views. You can even rent a paddleboat and explore the vineyards from a different perspective, gliding on the lake surrounded by this captivating landscape.

Whether you're a wine enthusiast, a nature lover, or simply seeking a beautiful escape, the Lavaux vineyards are a must-visit.

Outdoor Activities

Hiking and Trekking in the Alps

the Alps! Home to soaring peaks, lush valleys, and breathtaking vistas, the Alps offer some of the most incredible hiking and trekking experiences in the world. Whether you're a seasoned adventurer or a casual walker, the Alps have something for everyone.

For the thrill-seekers:

- **The Haute Route:** This classic trek, stretching from Chamonix in France to Zermatt in Switzerland, is a challenging but rewarding experience. You'll traverse glaciers, climb high passes, and be rewarded with panoramic views of some of the most iconic peaks in the Alps, like the Matterhorn and Mont Blanc.

- **The Eiger Trail:** This challenging trail takes you past the infamous north face of the Eiger, one of the most difficult mountains to climb in the Alps. Be prepared for breathtaking views and a good dose of adrenaline.

For the moderate hikers:

- **The Tour du Mont Blanc:** This scenic trail circles the majestic Mont Blanc massif, offering stunning views and a variety of landscapes, from alpine meadows to forests and glaciers. Choose from shorter sections or tackle the entire loop for an unforgettable experience.
- **The Five Lakes Trail:** This moderate trail takes you past five beautiful lakes in the Lauterbrunnen valley, offering stunning scenery and plenty of opportunities for swimming and picnicking.

For the family-friendly:

- **The Aletsch Glacier Trail:** This easy trail takes you along the edge of the Aletsch Glacier, the largest glacier in Europe. It's a great option for families with young children, as the trail is well-maintained and offers stunning views.
- **The Panorama Trail in Grindelwald:** This scenic trail offers panoramic views of the surrounding mountains and valleys. It's a good option for families with young children, as the trail is mostly flat and easy to walk.

Tips for planning your hiking or trekking trip in the Alps:

- **Choose the right trail for your fitness level and experience.** The Alps offer trails for all levels of hikers, so be sure to do your research and choose a trail that is appropriate for you.

- **Be prepared for the weather.** The weather in the Alps can change quickly, so be sure to pack for all conditions. This includes rain gear, sunscreen, a hat, and warm layers of clothing.
- **Book your accommodation in advance, especially during peak season.** The Alps are a popular tourist destination, so it's important to book your accommodation in advance, especially if you're planning on hiking during peak season (July and August).
- **Hire a guide if you're not experienced.** If you're not familiar with the Alps or are planning on tackling a challenging trail, it's a good idea to hire a guide. They can help you plan your route, navigate the trails, and ensure your safety.

With its stunning scenery, diverse trails, and rich culture, the Alps offer an unforgettable hiking and trekking experience for everyone. So lace up your boots, pack your bags, and get ready to explore this incredible mountain range!

Lake Geneva Boat Cruises

Lake Geneva, a shimmering expanse of blue nestled amidst the majestic peaks of the Alps, beckons with its undeniable charm. And what better way to experience its beauty than by embarking on a scenic cruise?

Lake Geneva boat cruises offer a unique perspective on the region, allowing you to soak in the breathtaking scenery, fascinating history, and vibrant culture from the comfort of the water.

A Plethora of Options:

Whether you're seeking a leisurely sightseeing excursion, a romantic evening cruise, or a themed event like a delicious brunch or dinner cruise, there's a Lake Geneva boat cruise that perfectly suits your desires.

- **Full Lake Cruise:** Embark on a comprehensive tour that encompasses the entire expanse of Lake Geneva. Marvel at the charming towns and villages dotting the shoreline, from the picturesque vineyards of Lavaux to the vibrant city of Geneva. Learn about the region's rich history and hidden gems as you cruise past iconic landmarks like Château de Chillon.
- **Lunch or Dinner Cruise:** Elevate your experience with a delightful lunch or dinner cruise. Savor exquisite culinary creations prepared by onboard chefs while enjoying the captivating sights and sounds of the lake. Imagine the gentle breeze carrying the scent of delicious food as you take in the stunning scenery – a truly unforgettable combination.
- **Special Event Cruises:** Throughout the year, Lake Geneva comes alive with various special events, and themed cruises reflect this vibrancy. Immerse yourself in the festive spirit of a Christmas market cruise, tap your foot to the rhythm of a live music cruise, or witness the dazzling spectacle of a fireworks cruise, creating memories that will last a lifetime.

Beyond the Cruise:

Your Lake Geneva adventure doesn't end after the cruise disembarks. Explore the charming towns and villages that line the shore, each offering a unique character and rich history. Sample local delicacies at cafes and restaurants, browse through quaint shops, or simply relax and soak up the atmosphere.

Planning Your Cruise:

- **Seasonality:** Lake Geneva boat cruises operate throughout the year, with the most extensive options available during the peak season (April to October).
- **Booking:** Booking your cruise in advance, especially during peak season, is recommended to secure your desired date and time.

- **Duration:** Cruise durations vary depending on the chosen option, ranging from short sightseeing tours to multi-hour lunch or dinner cruises.
- **Accessibility:** Most cruises are accessible to individuals with disabilities, but it's always recommended to check with the specific cruise operator beforehand.

Cycling Routes

Switzerland is a cyclist's paradise, offering a diverse range of routes catering to all experience levels and preferences. From challenging climbs in the alps to scenic lakeside rides, there's something for everyone to enjoy. Here are a few popular options:

For the thrill-seekers:

- **The Grand Colombier:** This iconic climb, nicknamed the "roof of the Jura," boasts breathtaking views and challenging switchbacks. It's a must-do for experienced cyclists seeking a test of their endurance.

For the scenic lovers:

- **Lake Geneva Perimeter Route:** This leisurely route circles the entire Lake Geneva, offering stunning lake and mountain views. You can choose to cycle the entire route in sections or complete the loop in a few days.
- **Emmental Valley:** Cycle through the rolling hills and charming villages of the Emmental Valley, known for its cheese production. Stop by a local cheesemaker to sample the region's famous Emmentaler cheese.

For the family-friendly:

- **Rhine River Route:** This mostly flat route follows the Rhine River from Andermatt to Basel, offering scenic countryside views and opportunities to explore charming towns along the way.

- **La Suisse à Velo Route 6:** This easy route connects Lausanne and Neuchâtel, following the shores of Lake Neuchâtel and offering stunning lake views. It's a great option for families with children.

Beyond the routes:

- **E-bikes:** E-bikes are a popular option in Switzerland, especially for those tackling challenging climbs or wanting a more relaxed cycling experience. Many rental shops offer e-bikes, allowing you to explore the diverse landscapes with ease.
- **Public transportation:** Combining cycling with public transportation is a great way to explore different regions of Switzerland. You can cycle one way and take the train back, allowing you to cover more ground and avoid challenging climbs.

No matter your cycling style or experience level, Switzerland has the perfect route waiting for you. So, grab your bike, hit the road, and experience the beauty of Switzerland on two wheels!

Water Sports (Kayaking, Stand-Up Paddleboarding)

While Montreux doesn't have a large lake within the town itself, it's situated on the shores of the vast Lake Geneva, opening up a variety of options for kayaking and stand-up paddleboarding. Here are some possibilities:

Kayaking:

- **Explore the Montreux Lakeside:** Paddle along the charming Montreux lakeside promenade, taking in the stunning views of the mountains and the bustling atmosphere of the town. You might even spot the iconic Freddie Mercury statue along the way!

- **Venture to nearby Vevey:** Kayak from Montreux towards the neighboring town of Vevey, enjoying the beautiful scenery and exploring the historic town center from a different perspective.

Stand-up paddleboarding (SUP):

- **Sunrise SUP sessions:** Start your day with a serene SUP session on Lake Geneva, witnessing the breathtaking sunrise paint the sky with vibrant colors while enjoying the tranquility of the calm waters.
- **Sunset SUP tours:** Experience the magic of Montreux as the sun dips below the horizon. Join a guided SUP tour that allows you to witness the stunning sunset views and the town lights reflecting on the water.

Additional options:

- **Guided tours:** Several companies offer guided kayaking and SUP tours in Montreux, providing equipment, instruction, and insights into the local area.
- **SUP yoga classes:** Combine SUP with some mindfulness by joining a SUP yoga class on the calm waters of Lake Geneva, offering a unique way to connect with your body and nature.

Remember, safety always comes first. Check weather conditions before heading out and consider taking lessons if you're new to water sports. With a little preparation, you can experience the beauty of Montreux from a refreshing and unique perspective!

Skiing and Snowboarding (winter season)

As Montreux sits nestled on the shores of Lake Geneva at a lower altitude, it doesn't have its own ski slopes. But fret not, fellow snow enthusiast! Montreux transforms into a winter wonderland gateway to several fantastic ski resorts, offering slopes for all levels. Here's what awaits you during the winter season:

Nearby Ski Resorts:

- **Rochers-de-Naye:** Just a short train ride from Montreux, Rochers-de-Naye offers breathtaking panoramic views and a small ski area with beginner and intermediate slopes. Perfect for families or those wanting a picturesque introduction to skiing or snowboarding.
- **Les Diablerets:** Renowned for its challenging terrain and stunning views, Les Diablerets is a paradise for experienced skiers and snowboarders. It's part of the extensive "Les Portes du Soleil" ski area, offering over 600km of slopes.
- **Gstaad:** This world-famous resort village offers a luxurious ambience and a variety of slopes catering to all skill levels, making it ideal for families and experienced skiers alike.
- **Villars-Gryon:** This interconnected ski area boasts diverse slopes, snow parks, and family-friendly activities, making it a popular choice for a complete winter vacation experience.

Beyond the slopes:

- **Après-ski:** After a day carving turns on the slopes, unwind and soak in the lively après-ski scene in Montreux. Cozy up in charming cafes, indulge in delicious fondue at a traditional restaurant, or enjoy live music and vibrant nightlife.
- **Christmas markets:** Immerse yourself in the festive spirit by visiting the Montreux Christmas Market, a magical wonderland adorned with twinkling lights, local crafts, and delicious treats.

Planning your winter escape:

- **Accommodation:** Book your accommodation well in advance, especially during peak season (December to February).
- **Equipment rentals:** Several shops in Montreux offer ski and snowboard equipment rentals.
- **Lift tickets:** Purchase your lift tickets online or at the ski resort ticket office.
- **Transportation:** Public transportation options are readily available to connect you to nearby ski resorts.

So, pack your winter gear, dust off your skis or snowboard, and get ready to experience the magic of winter sports in Montreux and its surrounding areas!

Dining and Cuisine

Swiss Cuisine and Specialty Dishes

Swiss cuisine is a delicious tapestry of regional specialties woven together by fresh, local ingredients and centuries-old traditions. From the iconic cheese fondue to hearty stews and delectable pastries, Swiss food is sure to tantalize your taste buds and offer a unique culinary experience.

Iconic Dishes:

- **Cheese Fondue:** The undisputed king of Swiss cuisine, fondue is a communal dish made with melted cheese, typically Gruyère, Vacherin Fribourgeois, or Emmental. Dip bread cubes, potatoes, or vegetables into the warm, gooey cheese and savor the rich and creamy flavor.
- **Raclette:** Another quintessential Swiss dish, raclette features melted cheese scraped from a wheel onto melted onions and potatoes. You can enjoy it as the main course or paired with charcuterie and pickles.

- **Rösti:** This savory potato dish is a staple in Switzerland. Grated potatoes are fried until golden brown and crispy, creating a comforting and flavorful side dish or vegetarian main course.

Regional Specialties:

- **Zürcher Geschnetzeltes:** This dish from Zurich features thinly sliced veal or pork cooked in a creamy mushroom sauce with white wine and rösti on the side.
- **Älplermagronen:** This hearty dish from Central Switzerland translates to "Alpine macaroni." It's a delectable mix of potatoes, macaroni, cheese, cream, and roasted onions, offering a comforting and filling meal.
- **Bündnerfleisch:** This air-dried meat specialty from Graubünden is made from beef and seasoned with various spices. It's typically enjoyed thinly sliced as an appetizer or snack.
- **Basler Leckerli:** These delicious honey cookies are a specialty of Basel. They're made with flour, honey, almonds, candied fruit, and spices, offering a unique and flavorful treat.
- **Birchermüesli:** This healthy breakfast option originated in Switzerland and has gained international popularity. It's a mixture of rolled oats, nuts, seeds, dried fruits, and yogurt, offering a nutritious and energizing start to your day.

Sweet Treats:

- **Swiss Chocolate:** Switzerland is renowned for its high-quality chocolate, and no culinary exploration would be complete without indulging in its rich and smooth flavors. From milk chocolate to dark chocolate with various fillings and nuts, the choices are endless.

- **Zuger Kirschtorte:** This cherry tart from the town of Zug is a delectable dessert featuring layers of cherry-infused kirsch liqueur, sponge cake, and butter cream.
- **Wähe:** This savory or sweet tart is a versatile dish popular across Switzerland. The base is typically made with flaky pastry, and the fillings can range from vegetables and cheese to fruits and jams.

Tips for Savoring Swiss Cuisine:

- **Explore local restaurants:** Look for restaurants with traditional menus to experience authentic Swiss flavors.
- **Visit farmers markets:** Immerse yourself in the local food scene by browsing farmers markets and sampling fresh produce and regional specialties.
- **Take a cooking class:** Learn the secrets of Swiss cuisine by participating in a cooking class and unlocking the culinary heritage of the region.

So, embark on a delicious journey through Switzerland, savor its iconic dishes, and discover the unique flavors that each region has to offer. The culinary delights await!

Fondue and Raclette Restaurants

As the weather cools and the snow falls, there's nothing quite like warming up with a delicious serving of fondue or raclette. Montreux offers a delightful selection of restaurants specializing in these classic Swiss dishes, ensuring a memorable culinary experience. Here are a few highly-rated options to tantalize your taste buds:

1. Restaurant Le Museum: Renowned for its traditional Swiss fare and warm ambiance, Restaurant Le Museum is a local favorite for both fondue and raclette.

Savor the rich and creamy cheese melted to perfection, accompanied by crusty bread, vegetables, and meats.

Address: Rue de la Gare 40, 1820 Montreux, Switzerland

2. La Fromagerie: Nestled in the charming village of Leysin, just a short drive from Montreux, La Fromagerie offers a delightful fondue experience. Choose from a variety of traditional and innovative fondue options, all prepared with the freshest local cheeses.

Address: Rue du Village 7, 1854 Leysin, Switzerland

3. Caveau des Vignerons: This charming restaurant boasts a cozy atmosphere and an extensive menu featuring both fondue and raclette. They also offer a delightful selection of local wines, perfectly complementing the rich cheeses.

Address: Rue Industrielle 30 bis, 1820 Montreux, Switzerland

4. Le Globe Montreux, Café Brasserie: While not solely dedicated to fondue and raclette, Le Globe Montreux offers a delightful selection of these Swiss specialties alongside other delectable dishes. Enjoy the warm and inviting atmosphere while indulging in these classic winter favorites.

Address: Avenue du Théâtre 4, 1820 Montreux, Switzerland

5. Cafe du Grutli: This charming cafe offers a cozy setting and a menu featuring both traditional and contemporary Swiss dishes. Their fondue and raclette are prepared with high-quality ingredients, ensuring a delicious and authentic experience.

Address: Grand' Rue 83, 1820 Montreux, Switzerland

Beyond the Restaurants:

For a truly unique fondue experience, consider indulging in a "fondue moitié-moitié." This traditional way of enjoying fondue involves dipping bread into a pot of cheese divided into Gruyère and Vacherin Fribourgeois, offering a delightful contrast of flavors and textures.

No matter your preference, Montreux offers a variety of restaurants and experiences to satisfy your fondue and raclette cravings. So, gather your friends and family, and embark on a culinary journey through the heart of Swiss cheese culture!

Lakeside Dining

Montreux, nestled on the shores of majestic Lake Geneva, offers a unique opportunity to combine the pleasure of fine dining with breathtaking views. From casual cafes to elegant restaurants, a diverse array of lakeside establishments cater to different tastes and budgets.

Casual with a View:

- **Le Deck:** This vibrant cafe-restaurant boasts a stunning lakeside terrace, perfect for enjoying a leisurely lunch or a refreshing drink while basking in the sun and admiring the panoramic views. They offer a variety of light bites, salads, pizzas, and refreshing cocktails. **Address:** Route de la Corniche 4, 1070 Puidoux-Chexbres, Switzerland
- **La Rouvenaz:** This charming restaurant, situated near the Chateau de Chillon, provides a delightful terrace overlooking the lake. Their menu features traditional Swiss dishes, fresh fish, and regional specialties, all prepared with seasonal ingredients. **Address:** Route de Villeneuve 130, 1820 Montreux, Switzerland

Fine Dining by the Lake:

- **Restaurant La Terrasse:** Perched on the Montreux Palace hotel rooftop, Restaurant La Terrasse offers an unparalleled dining experience. Savor exquisite French cuisine paired with exceptional wines while enjoying breathtaking panoramic views of the lake and the surrounding mountains. **Address:** Avenue Claude Nobs 2, 1820 Montreux, Switzerland
- **L'Hôtel Byron:** This luxurious hotel's elegant restaurant, Le Gastronomique, features innovative and modern cuisine prepared with fresh, seasonal ingredients. Indulge in a gourmet experience complemented by impeccable service and stunning lakeside views. **Address:** Avenue Eugène Yersin 13, 1820 Montreux, Switzerland

Hidden Gems:

- **Le Coucou:** This charming cafe, tucked away in a small alleyway, offers a cozy setting and a delightful selection of homemade pastries, sandwiches, and light meals. The terrace provides a glimpse of the lake, creating a charming ambiance for a casual lunch or coffee break. **Address:** Rue du Marché 4, 1820 Montreux, Switzerland
- **Auberge de la Tour:** Located in the nearby village of Veytaux, this traditional auberge offers a unique dining experience. Enjoy delicious local specialties and regional wines in a rustic setting with a charming lakeside terrace. **Address:** Route de Blonay 16, 1820 Veytaux, Switzerland

Tips for Lakeside Dining:

- **Reservations:** Particularly for popular restaurants during peak season (summer and winter), making reservations in advance is recommended.
- **Dress code:** While most lakeside restaurants are casual, some finer establishments might have a dress code. It's always best to check beforehand.

- **Outdoor seating:** If the weather permits, opt for a table on the terrace to fully enjoy the stunning lakeside views.

With its diverse selection of restaurants and captivating scenery, Montreux offers a delightful experience for those seeking to combine stunning views with delectable cuisine. So, whether you're looking for a casual lunch with a view or a fine dining experience in a luxurious setting, the lakeside options in Montreux are sure to tantalize your taste buds and leave you with lasting memories.

Local Markets and Food Festivals

Beyond its captivating scenery and tourist attractions, boasts a vibrant market scene and a calendar peppered with delightful food festivals. These events offer a unique window into the local culture, allowing you to sample regional specialties and discover hidden culinary gems.

Local Markets:

- **Montreux Christmas Market:** Held annually from late November to December, this charming market transforms the lakeside into a winter wonderland. Stroll through the festive stalls adorned with twinkling lights, browse handcrafted ornaments, and savor traditional treats like mulled wine, roasted chestnuts, and local cheeses.
- **Town Market:** Held every Tuesday and Saturday mornings, this bustling market offers a glimpse into the local way of life. Explore stalls overflowing with fresh produce, regional cheeses, locally baked bread, and unique souvenirs.

Food Festivals:

- **Montreux Jazz Festival (July):** While primarily focused on music, this world-renowned festival also features a vibrant food village. Savor

international cuisine from various vendors alongside the musical performances, creating a unique festival experience.
- **Fête des Vignerons (Winegrowers' Festival):** Held every 20-25 years, this UNESCO-listed festival is a vibrant celebration of local winemaking traditions. Witness colorful parades, folk music, and food stalls showcasing regional specialties paired with the celebrated wines of the Lavaux vineyards.
- **Chocolate Festival in Vevey (March):** This delightful festival, held in the neighboring town of Vevey, is a paradise for chocolate lovers. Explore booths showcasing Swiss chocolate from renowned brands and local artisans, participate in chocolate-making workshops, and indulge in decadent sweet treats.

Beyond the Fairs and Festivals:

- **Local Shops:** Montreux boasts charming shops offering regional products like local cheeses, cured meats, and artisanal jams.
- **Farm Visits:** For a truly immersive experience, consider visiting a local farm to witness traditional cheesemaking or sample fresh produce straight from the source.

Tips for Enjoying Local Markets and Food Festivals:

- **Bring cash:** While many vendors accept cards, having cash is recommended, especially at smaller stalls.
- **Arrive early:** Popular events can get crowded, so arriving early is recommended to avoid long lines and ensure you get your hands on the best offerings.
- **Embrace the experience:** Don't be afraid to try new things! Sample unfamiliar dishes and ask local vendors about their products to gain a deeper understanding of the regional cuisine.

By delving into the local markets and participating in food festivals, you can add a unique cultural dimension to your trip to Montreux, savoring its flavors and traditions beyond the typical tourist experience.

Shopping

Swiss Watches and Chocolate

Switzerland is renowned for two iconic products that have captivated the world for centuries: **exquisite Swiss watches and delectable Swiss chocolate**. These two seemingly unrelated items share a surprising connection, both deeply rooted in Swiss culture and tradition.

Swiss Watches: A Legacy of Precision and Innovation

For over 500 years, Switzerland has been at the forefront of watchmaking, establishing a reputation for unparalleled **precision, craftsmanship, and innovation**. The intricate mechanisms and meticulous attention to detail found in Swiss watches are a testament to the skill and dedication of Swiss watchmakers, passed down through generations.

Famous Swiss Watch Brands:

- **Rolex:** A symbol of luxury and status, Rolex is one of the most recognizable watch brands globally, known for its iconic Oyster and Daytona models.
- **Omega:** Renowned for its Speedmaster model, the first watch worn on the moon, Omega is another leading name in Swiss watchmaking, known for its advanced technology and timeless designs.
- **Patek Philippe:** A pioneer in complications and high-end watchmaking, Patek Philippe is known for its exquisite craftsmanship and heritage,

creating some of the most valuable and sought-after timepieces in the world.
- **Swatch:** A brand that revolutionized the watch industry by making stylish and affordable timepieces accessible to everyone, Swatch continues to push boundaries with its innovative and colorful designs.

Swiss Chocolate: A Symphony of Flavor and Indulgence

Switzerland's love affair with chocolate dates back to the 17th century. Today, Swiss chocolate is synonymous with **quality, richness, and unique flavor profiles**. The Swiss take pride in using the finest ingredients, traditional techniques, and rigorous quality control to create a truly indulgent experience.

Famous Swiss Chocolate Brands:

- **Lindt:** Known for its smooth, creamy texture and iconic gold packaging, Lindt is a global favorite, offering a variety of chocolate bars, truffles, and pralines.
- **Toblerone:** This triangular-shaped chocolate bar with nougat and honey is another iconic Swiss brand, recognized for its unique flavor and packaging.
- **Ferrero Rocher:** While not technically Swiss, Ferrero Rocher has a large production facility in Switzerland and is widely considered a Swiss chocolate brand. These individual chocolates with a crunchy hazelnut center, covered in milk chocolate and wafer, are a favorite worldwide.
- **Läderach:** A family-owned company with a long history, Läderach is known for its high-quality chocolate bars, truffles, and other confectionery items, made with fresh, natural ingredients.

The Unexpected Connection: A Shared Commitment to Excellence

While seemingly unrelated, Swiss watches and chocolate share a surprising connection. Both industries are deeply rooted in **Swiss tradition, a commitment to excellence, and meticulous attention to detail**. The same dedication to quality and craftsmanship that goes into creating a world-class watch is also evident in the production of the finest Swiss chocolate.

A Delightful Combination: Indulge in Both Worlds

For visitors to Switzerland, experiencing both Swiss watches and chocolate is a must. Whether you marvel at the intricate mechanisms of a timepiece at a watch museum or savor the rich flavors of a decadent chocolate bar, you'll gain a deeper appreciation for the **uncompromising quality, rich heritage, and unique character** that define these iconic Swiss products.

Souvenirs and Gifts

Montreux offers a delightful selection of souvenirs and gifts, allowing you to bring back a piece of the city's charm and a reminder of your memorable trip. Here are some ideas to inspire you:

For the Foodie:

- **Swiss Chocolate:** As mentioned previously, Swiss chocolate is a must-have souvenir. From renowned brands like Lindt and Toblerone to local artisan chocolatiers, there's something for every taste bud.
- **Cheese:** Switzerland boasts a diverse range of cheeses, each with its own unique flavor and texture. Consider bringing back a selection of local favorites like Gruyère, Vacherin Fribourgeois, or Emmental.
- **Local Jams and Honey:** Delight your taste buds with locally-made jams and honey, perfect for spreading on bread or pairing with cheese.

For the Home:

- **Cowbells:** A classic Swiss souvenir, cowbells come in various sizes and are a charming reminder of the country's vibrant alpine culture.
- **Wooden Crafts:** From hand-carved figurines to decorative boxes, Swiss wooden crafts are beautiful and functional souvenirs.
- **Textiles:** Bring back a piece of Swiss tradition with a cozy knitted scarf, hat, or blanket made from high-quality wool.

For the Fashionista:

- **Swiss Army Knife:** A versatile and practical tool, the Swiss Army Knife is a timeless souvenir that combines functionality with a touch of Swiss heritage.
- **Swiss Watches:** While high-end Swiss watches might not be for everyone, there are a variety of affordable and stylish options available, allowing you to own a piece of Swiss watchmaking tradition.
- **Jewelry:** From delicate pieces featuring traditional Swiss motifs to modern designs, Swiss jewelry offers something for every style.

For the Memory Maker:

- **Montreux Jazz Festival Merchandise:** If you visit during the festival, don't miss the opportunity to pick up a t-shirt, cap, or other souvenir commemorating the event.
- **Freddie Mercury Statue Replica:** A miniature replica of the iconic statue of Freddie Mercury, located on the lakeside promenade, is a unique and meaningful souvenir for Queen fans.
- **Postcards and Magnets:** These classic souvenirs are a budget-friendly way to capture your memories of Montreux and share them with loved ones back home.

Where to Find Souvenirs:

- **Gift Shops:** Montreux has a variety of gift shops offering a wide selection of souvenirs catering to all tastes and budgets.
- **Markets:** The Montreux Christmas Market and the Town Market are great places to find unique and handmade souvenirs from local artisans.
- **Department Stores:** Department stores like Manor and Globus offer a wider selection of souvenirs, including clothing, watches, and chocolates.

Remember: When choosing souvenirs, consider supporting local businesses and artisans to ensure your purchases contribute to the local economy and preserve the traditional crafts of the region.

Boutique Shops and Artisanal Crafts

Nestled amidst the captivating scenery of Lake Geneva, Montreux offers a delightful experience beyond its natural beauty. For those seeking unique treasures and locally crafted keepsakes, the city boasts a charming selection of boutique shops and artisanal havens.

Embark on a Shopping Spree in Montreux's Boutiques:

- **La Chatte:** This quaint shop, located at Av. des Alpes 33, is a treasure trove of secondhand books and unique gifts. Whether you're a bibliophile seeking a rare find or searching for a quirky souvenir, La Chatte is sure to have something special for you.
- **Montreux Knitting Sir S.A.:** Immerse yourself in the world of exquisite knitwear at Montreux Knitting Sir S.A., located at Av. du Casino 55. From luxurious cashmere scarves to cozy woolen hats, this shop offers high-quality pieces crafted with meticulous attention to detail.
- **Laines:** Discover a haven for yarn enthusiasts at Laines, situated at Grand' Rue 16. This shop boasts an extensive selection of yarns in various colors and textures, perfect for knitting or crocheting your own creations. They

also offer workshops and classes for those interested in learning the art of yarn crafts.

Unearth Local Treasures at Artisanal Markets:

- **Marché de Noël de Montreux (Montreux Christmas Market):** Held annually from late November to December, this enchanting Christmas market transforms the lakeside into a winter wonderland. Browse through stalls adorned with twinkling lights, overflowing with handcrafted ornaments, local delicacies, and unique artisanal creations.
- **Marché de la Ville (Town Market):** Immerse yourself in the local way of life at the bustling Town Market, held every Tuesday and Saturday mornings in the heart of Montreux. Explore stalls brimming with fresh produce, regional cheeses, and handcrafted souvenirs, like locally made jewelry, pottery, and artwork.

Beyond the Shops and Markets:

- **Galerie LJ Art:** Immerse yourself in the local art scene at Galerie LJ Art, located at Rue du Marché 4. This gallery showcases works by established and emerging Swiss artists, offering a glimpse into the artistic expressions of the region.
- **L'Atelier du Chocolatier:** Indulge your sweet tooth and witness the art of chocolate making at L'Atelier du Chocolatier, located at Rue du Théâtre 4. This charming shop offers delectable chocolates crafted using traditional methods and high-quality ingredients, perfect for satisfying your cravings or gifting to loved ones.

As you explore the charming streets of Montreux, keep an eye out for hidden gems tucked away in alleyways and side streets. These smaller boutiques and workshops often showcase the work of local artisans, offering a unique selection of handcrafted items and personalized experiences.

Whether you're searching for a one-of-a-kind souvenir, a statement piece of clothing, or simply a glimpse into the local culture, Montreux's boutique shops and artisanal havens offer a delightful treasure hunt for every visitor.

Nightlife and Entertainment

Bars and Pubs

Montreux offers a vibrant tapestry of after-dark experiences catering to diverse tastes. From traditional Irish havens to chic cocktail havens, you're sure to find the perfect spot to unwind and enjoy an evening on the town.

For the Pub Enthusiast:

- **Barrel Oak (Av. des Alpes 37, Montreux):** This lively pub boasts a warm welcome and classic Irish pub atmosphere. Enjoy a pint of Guinness, indulge in traditional pub fare like fish and chips, and catch live music on select nights. (Open: Mon-Thu 11:00 AM - 1:00 AM; Fri: 11:00 AM - 2:00 AM; Sat: 12:00 PM - 2:00 AM; Sun: 12:00 AM - 12:00 AM)
- **The Mad Cow (Rue du Casino 21, Montreux):** Offering a spacious terrace overlooking the lake and a relaxed atmosphere, this pub boasts a wide selection of beers, including local Swiss brews and international favorites, alongside pub classics. (Open: Daily from 11:00 AM to 1:00 AM)

For the Cocktail Connoisseur:

- **Funky Claude's Bar (Av. Claude Nobs 2, Montreux):** Known for its innovative and creative cocktails, this stylish establishment is perfect for a sophisticated evening. Their talented bartenders craft unique concoctions

using fresh ingredients and premium spirits. (Open: Tue-Thu 6:00 PM - 2:00 AM; Fri-Sat 6:00 PM - 4:00 AM; Sun-Mon closed)
- **Le National (Quai du Petit-Chêne 16, Vevey):** Situated near Montreux in Vevey, Le National offers stunning lake views and an extensive cocktail menu. Sip on a classic Martini or try one of their signature creations while taking in the picturesque scenery. (Open: Sun-Thu 10:00 AM - 1:00 AM; Fri-Sat 10:00 AM - 2:00 AM)

For an Unforgettable Night:

- **Taboo Bar & Lounge (Pl. du Marché 12, Montreux):** This vibrant establishment offers shisha pipes, cocktails, and music, creating a diverse crowd and lively atmosphere. (Open: Daily from 9:00 PM to 4:00 AM)
- **The Docks (Rue de la Navigation 10, Montreux):** This unique venue combines a bar, restaurant, and bowling alley. Enjoy a delicious meal, challenge your friends to a game of bowling, and unwind with a refreshing drink. (Open: Sun-Thu 11:30 AM - 12:00 AM; Fri-Sat 11:30 AM - 2:00 AM)

Unveiling Hidden Gems:

Explore Montreux's vibrant nightlife beyond the main streets. Discover local favorites with unique personalities tucked away in alleys and side streets.

Live Music: Many bars and pubs host live music nights, featuring local and international musicians playing various genres. Check local listings or ask at the bars to discover who's playing during your visit.

Tips for Enjoying Montreux's Nightlife:

- **Dress code:** While most venues are casual, some upscale establishments might have a dress code. Check beforehand if unsure.

- **Age restrictions:** The legal drinking age in Switzerland is 18. Be prepared to show ID if you look young.
- **Public transportation:** Montreux has a good public transportation system, allowing you to get around safely and avoid driving under the influence.

Whether you seek a lively pub atmosphere, a sophisticated cocktail bar, or a unique night out, Montreux's diverse selection of bars and pubs guarantees a memorable evening for every visitor. So, raise a glass, unwind, and experience the vibrant nightlife scene in this charming Swiss town.

Live Music Venues

Montreux, nestled on the shores of Lake Geneva, isn't just about breathtaking scenery and delicious cheese. It also boasts a vibrant live music scene, catering to diverse genres and tastes. Whether you're a jazz aficionado, a rock enthusiast, or simply enjoy a lively atmosphere, you'll find the perfect venue to tap your feet and groove to the music.

Legendary Stages:

- **Montreux Jazz Café (Av. Claude Nobs 2, Montreux):** This iconic venue, located within the Fairmont Le Montreux Palace hotel, is a must-visit for any music lover. While primarily known for hosting jazz legends during the Montreux Jazz Festival, the cafe regularly features live performances by talented local and international artists throughout the year. (Open: Daily from 11:30 AM to 10:30 PM)

Beyond Jazz:

- **Funky Claude's Bar (Av. Claude Nobs 2, Montreux):** Housed within the same building as the Montreux Jazz Café, Funky Claude's Bar offers a

more intimate and contemporary setting for live music. From emerging local bands to established artists playing various genres like rock, funk, and pop, there's always something new to discover here. (Open: Thurs-Sat, live music from 6 PM)
- **The Docks (Rue de la Navigation 10, Montreux):** While primarily a bar and restaurant, The Docks frequently hosts live music nights featuring local bands and DJs. The diverse music selection and lively atmosphere make it a popular spot for a fun night out. (Open: Sun-Thu 11:30 AM - 12:00 AM; Fri-Sat 11:30 AM - 2:00 AM)

Hidden Gems:

- **Le Palais (Rue du Théâtre 4, Montreux):** This intimate and historic theatre occasionally hosts live music concerts, often featuring classical, jazz, and world music performances. While live music events are not as frequent as in other venues, the unique setting and talented artists make it a worthwhile experience. (Open: Varies depending on the event)
- **Petit Palais (Av. du Casino 2, Montreux):** This smaller venue, located within the Casino Barrière Montreux, sometimes hosts live music events, ranging from jazz and blues to pop and rock. Check the casino's website for upcoming events. (Open: Varies depending on the event)

Finding Your Groove:

- **Local Listings:** Explore websites and social media pages of bars, clubs, and cultural centers in Montreux to discover upcoming live music events.
- **Ask Around:** Chat with locals, hotel staff, or staff at bars and cafes for recommendations on live music venues and events based on your preferred genre.

Tips for Enjoying Live Music in Montreux:

- **Check the schedule:** Plan your visit around live music events happening during your stay.
- **Dress code:** Most venues have a casual dress code, but it's always a good idea to check beforehand if unsure.
- **Respect the performers:** Arrive on time, refrain from talking loudly during performances, and show appreciation for the musicians.

With its diverse venues, talented artists, and passionate audience, Montreux offers a unique live music experience for every visitor. So, put on your dancing shoes, grab some friends, and get ready to enjoy the vibrant music scene in this charming Swiss town.

Casino Barrière de Montreux

Also known as the Montreux Casino, is a historic landmark and entertainment complex located on the shores of Lake Geneva in Montreux, Switzerland.

History and Significance:

Built in 1881, the casino has played a significant role in the town's cultural and economic development. It has hosted numerous renowned artists and events over the years, including the legendary Montreux Jazz Festival, which has been held at the casino since 1967. The casino was accidentally set on fire in 1971 during a Frank Zappa concert, inspiring the iconic Deep Purple song "Smoke on the Water."

What it Offers:

Today, the Casino Barrière de Montreux offers a range of entertainment options, including:

- **Casino:** Featuring over 350 slot machines, 18 table games, and a poker room, the casino caters to both casual and experienced gamers.
- **Restaurants:** The complex houses several restaurants, including the renowned Le Fouquet's, offering French cuisine, and La Mamma, specializing in Italian dishes.
- **Bars:** The casino boasts several bars, including L'Escadrille Bar, offering stunning views of Lake Geneva, and the trendy Funky Claude's Bar, known for its innovative cocktails.
- **Shows and Events:** The casino regularly hosts various shows, concerts, and events throughout the year, catering to diverse interests.

Beyond Gambling:

While the casino is a major attraction, the complex also offers a variety of experiences beyond gambling. Visitors can enjoy:

- **Exhibitions:** The casino occasionally hosts art exhibitions showcasing local and international artists.
- **Guided tours:** Take a guided tour of the casino to learn about its history, architecture, and iconic events.
- **Stunning location:** The casino's location on the shores of Lake Geneva offers breathtaking views and a picturesque setting.

Overall, the Casino Barrière de Montreux is a must-visit destination in Montreux, offering a unique blend of entertainment, history, and cultural significance.

Wellness and relaxation

Spa Resorts and Wellness Centers

Nestled amidst the captivating scenery of Lake Geneva, Montreux offers a haven for relaxation and rejuvenation beyond its natural beauty. For those seeking luxurious pampering and holistic wellness experiences, the town boasts an array of esteemed spa resorts and wellness centers.

Indulge in Luxurious Rejuvenation:

- **Le Mirador Resort & Spa:** Posh spa resort offering 2 restaurants, a cocktail lounge & an indoor pool, plus a gym & tennis. This renowned resort, perched high above Montreux in Chardonne, offers breathtaking panoramic views of the lake and the surrounding mountains.

- **Fairmont Le Montreux Palace:** Elegant hotel with lake & mountain views, offering elegant dining, trendy cocktails & a spa. This iconic hotel, located on the shores of Lake Geneva, features the renowned Willow Stream Spa, known for its extensive treatment menu and luxurious amenities.

- **Royal Plaza Montreux SA:** Polished rooms & suites in a high-end lakefront hotel offering a French restaurant & an upscale spa. This sophisticated hotel boasts the Cinq Mondes Spa, providing a unique journey through the world of wellness with treatments inspired by various cultures.

Embrace Holistic Wellness:

- **Le Baron Tavernier:** Refined quarters, some with lake views, in a premium property featuring a spa & 3 dining options. Located in Chexbres, this charming hotel features the La Source des Alpes Spa, offering a holistic approach to wellness with treatments focused on natural therapies and local products.

- **Eurotel Montreux:** Spa Hotel in Montreux. This contemporary hotel boasts a modern spa with an indoor pool, sauna, hammam, and a variety of wellness treatments.

- **Hôtel du Grand Lac Excelsior:** Situated in the heart of Montreux, the Hotel du Grand Lac Excelsior has a privileged location right on Lake Geneva. It offers free access to the spa, which features an indoor pool, sauna, hammam, and a relaxation area.

Unwind and Rejuvenate:

These are just a few of the exceptional spa resorts and wellness centers that Montreux offers. Whether you seek a luxurious escape, a holistic approach to well-being, or simply a moment of relaxation, you're sure to find the perfect sanctuary for your needs in this charming Swiss town.

Thermal Baths

Montreux,might not be home to traditional thermal baths in the sense of naturally occurring hot springs. However, the nearby town of Lavey-les-Bains, located about a 20-minute drive from Montreux, boasts the **Lavey Thermal Baths**, renowned for its warm, mineral-rich waters sourced from the mountains.

Warmth and Wellness:

- **Heated pools:** The Lavey Thermal Baths complex features a variety of indoor and outdoor pools with varying temperatures, catering to different preferences. The hottest pool boasts a temperature of $33°C$ ($91°F$), perfect for relaxation and muscle tension relief.
- **Mineral-rich waters:** The thermal waters at Lavey are naturally rich in minerals like calcium, magnesium, and sulfur, believed to offer various health benefits, including improved circulation, pain relief, and relaxation.
- **Spa treatments:** In addition to the bathing facilities, Lavey offers a comprehensive range of spa treatments, including massages, facials, and body wraps, to further enhance your wellness experience.

Beyond the Baths:

- **Saunas and hammams:** The complex also features saunas and hammams, providing additional relaxation and detoxification benefits.
- **Restaurants:** Several restaurants within the complex cater to various dietary needs, allowing you to enjoy a delicious meal after your spa session.
- **Accommodation:** Lavey offers a variety of accommodation options, from hotels to apartments, allowing you to extend your stay and fully immerse yourself in the thermal bath experience.

Planning Your Visit:

- **Open year-round:** The Lavey Thermal Baths are open year-round, making them a perfect destination for relaxation and rejuvenation any time of year.
- **Day trips or extended stays:** You can choose to visit the baths for a day trip from Montreux or book accommodation in Lavey for a longer stay.
- **Check the website:** Before your visit, check the official website of the Lavey Thermal Baths for current opening hours, pricing, and any special offers or events.

While Montreux itself may not have thermal baths, the Lavey Thermal Baths, located a short distance away, offer an exceptional thermal bath experience with its warm, mineral-rich waters, diverse spa treatments, and beautiful surroundings.

Yoga and Meditation Classes

Situated amidst the breathtaking scenery of Lake Geneva, this charming city offers a tranquil escape, not only for the eye but also for the mind and body. If you're seeking to deepen your yoga practice or explore the world of meditation, the city boasts an array of studios and options to suit your needs.

Immerse Yourself in Yoga:

- **Yogacenter By Patrick Nolfo (Av. du Casino 48):** Established in 1998, this renowned studio offers a diverse schedule of yoga classes catering to various levels and interests. From Hatha and Vinyasa to Yin and Restorative yoga, you're sure to find a class that aligns with your practice and goals. They also offer private lessons and workshops to further personalize your yoga journey.
- **YogaHome Women (Rle du Vuagnard 1):** Focusing on women's well-being, this cozy studio offers Hatha, Yin, and Vinyasa yoga classes, as well as Pilates and meditation sessions. They also organize special workshops and retreats, creating a supportive and empowering environment for women to connect with themselves and others.
- **Fairmont Le Montreux Palace Hotel (Av. Claude Nobs 2):** While not a dedicated yoga studio, the Fairmont Le Montreux Palace Hotel offers occasional yoga classes as part of their wellness activities. This can be a convenient option if you're staying at the hotel and want to maintain your practice during your trip.

Unwind with Meditation:

- **Apprentus - Yoga lessons (various locations):** This online platform connects you with experienced yoga teachers in the city who offer private yoga and meditation lessons in the comfort of your own accommodation or at a chosen location. This personalized approach allows you to tailor the session to your specific needs and preferences.
- **Guided meditations online:** While not physically located in the city, numerous online resources offer free and paid guided meditations on

various topics, allowing you to practice meditation in the privacy of your own space. Explore apps like Calm, Headspace, and Insight Timer to find guided meditations that resonate with you.

Finding the Perfect Fit:

- **Consider your experience level:** Whether you're a seasoned yogi or a complete beginner, choose a class or instructor that caters to your current practice and comfort level.
- **Explore different styles:** The city offers a variety of yoga styles. Try different classes to discover which style resonates most with you and your body.
- **Check the schedule and booking:** Contact the studios or visit their websites to check their class schedules, booking procedures, and pricing information.

Embrace the Tranquility:

With its beautiful setting and diverse options, the city provides the perfect environment to nurture your mind, body, and spirit through yoga and meditation. So, unwind, breathe deeply, and find your inner peace in this captivating haven.

Lakeside Relaxation Spots

This enchanting city provides a haven for relaxation and rejuvenation. Whether you seek a quiet corner to unwind with a book, a picturesque spot for a picnic lunch, or a vibrant atmosphere to people-watch, the city's lakeside boasts a variety of spots to suit your mood.

Unwind in Picturesque Tranquility:

- **Promenade sur les quais de Montreux:** This scenic walkway stretches along the lakeside, offering stunning panoramic views of Lake Geneva and the surrounding mountains. Lined with benches and shaded areas, it's the perfect place to take a leisurely stroll, soak in the fresh air, or simply relax and watch the world go by.
- **Parc des Roses:** Located near the Château de Chillon, this charming park boasts a vibrant display of roses in bloom during the summer months. With its tranquil atmosphere, manicured lawns, and shaded benches, it's a serene spot to escape the hustle and bustle and enjoy a moment of peace.
- **Les Jardins du Petit Château:** Nestled between the Casino Barrière de Montreux and the Hôtel du Parc, these charming gardens offer a peaceful haven amidst the city's vibrant atmosphere. With its beautiful flower beds, mature trees, and a small pond, it's a delightful spot to relax and disconnect from the outside world.

Embrace a Lively Atmosphere:

- **Montreux Beach (Blonay):** This popular beach, located just outside the city center, offers a vibrant atmosphere perfect for enjoying a picnic lunch, sunbathing, or taking a refreshing dip in the lake. With its volleyball courts, playground, and lakeside cafes, it's a lively spot for families and groups to relax and enjoy the sunshine.
- **Places de la Gare:** Located near the train station, this bustling square offers a lively atmosphere for people-watching. With its cafes, street performers, and occasional festivals, it's a vibrant spot to soak up the city's energy and enjoy a refreshing drink while watching the world go by.

A Lakeside Escape for Everyone:

These are just a few of the many lakeside relaxation spots the city has to offer. Whether you seek a tranquil escape or a vibrant atmosphere, there's a perfect spot along the lake to unwind, recharge, and create lasting memories in this charming Swiss city.

Day Trips from Montreux

Lausanne

Montreux is a fantastic spot, but if you're looking to explore beyond its beautiful shores, Lausanne is just a short train ride or scenic boat trip away. It's like a hidden gem waiting to be discovered!

Lausanne is steeped in history, with a charming old town and a massive cathedral that'll leave you speechless. Plus, there are amazing museums like the Musée de l'Élysée, which is a photographer's paradise, and the Olympic Museum, where you can delve into the history of the games.

But Lausanne isn't just about museums! The food scene is incredible, with everything from traditional Swiss fare like rösti and fondue to delicious international cuisine. And let's not forget the views! Lausanne sits on hills overlooking Lake Geneva, so stunning panoramas are guaranteed. You can even take a ride on the Lausanne Metro, one of the steepest funicular railways in Europe, for a truly unique experience.

So, if you're feeling adventurous and want to explore a charming city with a vibrant atmosphere, Lausanne is the perfect day trip from Montreux. Trust me, it won't disappoint!

Gruyères

Gruyères is a charming medieval town nestled in the heart of Switzerland, renowned for its namesake cheese and breathtaking scenery.

Imagine strolling through cobbled streets lined with colorful houses and traditional shops, all while surrounded by rolling green hills and the majestic peaks of the Fribourg Pre-Alps.

Here are some highlights that will make Gruyères a delightful day trip or weekend escape:

1. Gruyères Castle: This imposing 13th-century castle dominates the town and offers a fascinating glimpse into the region's history. Explore its ramparts, knights' hall, and exhibits showcasing art, architecture, and the cultural heritage of Gruyères.

2. Cheesemaking Experience: Immerse yourself in the world of Gruyère cheese by visiting a local cheese factory, like La Maison du Gruyère. Witness the traditional cheesemaking process, learn about the secrets behind its unique flavor, and savor samples of this delectable cheese.

3. Chocolate Delights: Switzerland is synonymous with chocolate, and Gruyères is no exception. Visit the Maison Cailler chocolate factory and embark on a journey through the history of Swiss chocolate making. Indulge in tastings and discover the delectable creations of this renowned chocolatier.

4. Scenic Walks and Hikes: The surrounding countryside offers a plethora of hiking trails catering to all levels. Breathe in the fresh Alpine air and admire the breathtaking panoramas as you explore the charming villages and rolling hills.

5. Fondue Feast: No trip to Gruyères is complete without indulging in a traditional cheese fondue. Savor this melted cheese dish accompanied by bread and local wine in a cozy restaurant, soaking up the warm ambiance and local flavors.

Beyond the Town:

- **Moléson:** For the adventurous, the nearby Moléson mountain offers stunning views and various activities, from hiking and biking in summer to skiing and snowboarding in winter. Take the cable car to the summit for breathtaking panoramas of the region.
- **Lake Gruyère:** This scenic lake offers opportunities for relaxation and recreation. Enjoy a boat trip, try your hand at fishing, or simply soak up the tranquility of the lakeside scenery.

Gruyères offers a delightful blend of history, culture, and natural beauty, making it a captivating destination for a memorable Swiss escape.

Glacier 3000

Glacier 3000 is a breathtaking mountain resort located in the Vaud Alps, Switzerland, offering stunning views, thrilling activities, and a unique alpine experience year-round. Whether you're a seasoned skier, a nature enthusiast, or simply seeking a picturesque escape, Glacier 3000 has something to offer everyone.

Reaching the Summit:

Soaring to an altitude of 3,000 meters (9,843 ft), Glacier 3000 is easily accessible by a two-stage cable car ride. The first section takes you from the valley station in Les Diablerets to Col de Sonalon, offering panoramic views of the surrounding mountains. The second section, a high-speed cable car known as "Cabrio," features open-air cabins, allowing you to fully immerse yourself in the breathtaking scenery as you ascend to the summit.

Winter Wonderland:

During the winter months, Glacier 3000 transforms into a skier's paradise, boasting 13 km (8.1 miles) of groomed pistes, catering to all levels, from gentle beginner slopes to challenging black runs. Freestyle enthusiasts can enjoy the expansive snowpark, while off-piste adventures await daring skiers and snowboarders.

Summer Activities:

Summer at Glacier 3000 offers a plethora of activities for every interest. Hike or bike through the scenic alpine trails, marvel at the panoramic views from the Peak Walk by Tissot, the world's first suspension bridge connecting two peaks, or take a thrilling ride on the Alpine Coaster, the highest toboggan run in the world.

More to Explore:

- **Glacier Caves:** Embark on a guided tour of the Glacier Caves, venturing deep into the heart of the mountain and into a world of glistening ice formations and hidden chambers.
- **Panoramic Restaurant:** Enjoy a delicious meal at the panoramic restaurant, "Le Kuklos," while taking in the breathtaking views of the surrounding Alpine landscape.
- **Events:** Throughout the year, Glacier 3000 hosts various events, from concerts and festivals to sporting competitions, adding an extra layer of excitement to your visit.

A Memorable Swiss Experience:

With its stunning scenery, diverse activities, and unique alpine experience, Glacier 3000 is an unforgettable destination for any Swiss adventure. So, pack your bags, grab your camera, and prepare to be awestruck by the beauty and wonder of this captivating mountain resort.

Montreux Riviera Cruise

The Montreux Riviera Cruise, offered by the Compagnie Générale de Navigation (CGN), is a delightful way to explore the scenic beauty and charming towns along the Swiss Riviera, the region bordering Lake Geneva.

The cruise offers various routes and durations, allowing you to tailor the experience to your preferences and time constraints. Some popular options include:

- **Riviera Tour (Lausanne - Vevey - Villeneuve):** This classic route takes you on a captivating journey, starting in Lausanne and passing by the charming towns of Vevey and Villeneuve. During the cruise, you can admire the breathtaking scenery, including the majestic peaks of the Dents du Midi and the rolling vineyards of Lavaux, a UNESCO World Heritage Site.
- **Lavaux Tour (Lausanne - Vevey - Lausanne):** This shorter route focuses on the Lavaux region, known for its picturesque vineyards and wine production. Enjoy stunning views of the terraced vineyards clinging to the hillsides and learn about the region's rich winemaking heritage.
- **Crossings**: CGN also offers various crossing options between different towns and villages on the Swiss and French shores of Lake Geneva, allowing you to explore the region at your own pace and create your own itinerary.

Highlights of the Montreux Riviera Cruise:

- **Relaxing and scenic journey:** Sit back, relax, and soak up the breathtaking beauty of the surrounding landscape as you glide across the crystal-clear waters of Lake Geneva.

- **Sightseeing opportunities:** The cruise allows you to admire the charming towns, historical landmarks, and stunning scenery of the Swiss Riviera from a unique perspective.
- **Onboard amenities:** Depending on the chosen route and vessel, you may have access to various onboard amenities, such as restaurants, bars, and sun decks, enhancing your cruising experience.
- **Audio guide:** Enhance your understanding of the region's history and landmarks by renting an audio guide available in multiple languages.

Planning Your Cruise:

- **Choose your route and duration:** Decide which route and duration best suit your interests and time constraints.
- **Check the schedule and book your tickets:** Visit the CGN website or local tourist information centers to check the current schedule and book your tickets in advance, especially during peak season.
- **Consider the weather:** The scenery is breathtaking year-round, but if you prefer warm weather and outdoor seating, consider a cruise during the spring or summer months.
- **Dress comfortably:** Pack comfortable shoes and clothing suitable for the weather conditions.

A Memorable Experience Awaits:

The Montreux Riviera Cruise offers a delightful and relaxing way to explore the beauty and charm of the Swiss Riviera. Whether you're a seasoned traveler or a first-time visitor, this cruise promises a memorable experience, leaving you with lasting memories of the stunning scenery and charming towns of this captivating region.

Practical Tips and Advice

Safety Tips

Montreux is a generally safe and welcoming city, known for its stunning scenery and relaxed atmosphere. However, as with any travel destination, it's always wise to be mindful of your surroundings and take some basic precautions to ensure a smooth and enjoyable trip. Here are some safety tips to keep in mind:

General Safety:

- **Be aware of your surroundings:** Pay attention to your belongings, especially in crowded areas like train stations and tourist attractions.
- **Carry your valuables safely:** Keep your wallet, passport, and other valuables secure in a money belt or a secure pocket. Avoid carrying large sums of cash.
- **Be cautious with pickpockets:** While uncommon, pickpocketing can occur in crowded areas. Remain vigilant and keep your belongings close to your body.
- **Beware of scams:** Unfortunately, scams can happen anywhere. Be cautious of individuals offering unsolicited services or deals that seem too good to be true.
- **Respect local customs and laws:** Familiarize yourself with local laws and customs to avoid any misunderstandings or disrespectful behavior.

Transportation:

- **Public transportation:** Montreux has a safe and efficient public transportation system. Validate your tickets before boarding, and be aware of your surroundings while waiting at bus stops or train stations.

- **Taxis:** Use licensed taxis and agree on the fare beforehand to avoid any disputes upon arrival.
- **Walking and cycling:** Montreux is a pedestrian-friendly city, and walking or cycling can be a great way to explore. When walking at night, stick to well-lit areas and main roads.
- **Hiking:** If venturing on hikes in the surrounding mountains, always plan your route carefully, check weather conditions, and inform someone of your plans. Consider carrying a map, compass, and appropriate gear.

Emergency Situations:

- **Emergency number:** In case of an emergency, dial 112 from any phone to reach emergency services.
- **First aid:** There are several pharmacies throughout the city where you can find basic first-aid supplies.
- **Health insurance:** Ensure you have adequate travel insurance to cover any medical emergencies or unexpected events during your trip.

Additional Tips:

- **Learn basic French phrases:** While English is understood by many locals, learning a few basic French phrases can enhance your communication and experience.
- **Download offline maps or language translation apps:** Having access to offline maps and a translation app can be helpful, especially if you get lost or need assistance communicating.
- **Drink responsibly:** While Montreux offers a vibrant nightlife, consume alcohol responsibly and avoid placing yourself in potentially risky situations.

By following these simple safety tips and remaining vigilant, you can ensure a safe and enjoyable trip to Montreux. Remember, the local people are friendly and welcoming, and most importantly, relax and have a fantastic time exploring this beautiful city!

Budgeting and Money Matters

Accommodation:

- **Accommodation options vary widely:** Montreux offers a diverse range of accommodation, from budget-friendly hostels and guesthouses to luxurious hotels with lakefront views. Research and compare prices to find an option that fits your budget and preferences.
- **Consider the location:** Staying closer to the city center allows easy access to attractions and public transport but might be pricier. Consider exploring options slightly outside the center for potentially better deals.
- **Book in advance:** Especially during peak season (summer and major events), booking your accommodation well in advance can secure better deals and avoid last-minute price surges.

Food:

- **Restaurant prices can vary:** Montreux offers various restaurants cater to diverse budgets. Fine dining establishments will naturally be more expensive than casual cafes or local eateries. Consider exploring options beyond the main tourist areas for potentially better value.
- **Self-catering:** Consider staying in accommodations with self-catering facilities like a kitchenette, allowing you to prepare some meals yourself and potentially save on dining costs.

- **Pick up groceries at local markets:** Local supermarkets and markets often offer fresh produce and groceries at more affordable prices compared to convenience stores or tourist-oriented shops.

Activities and Attractions:

- **Free and budget-friendly options:** Montreux boasts several free or affordable activities, such as strolling along the lakeside promenade, exploring the old town, visiting the Montreux Christmas Market (during the festive season), or picnicking in a park.
- **Purchase a Montreux Riviera Card:** This card offers free public transport within the region, discounts on various activities and attractions, and even free entry to some museums, potentially saving you money on transportation and sightseeing costs.
- **Plan your itinerary and prioritize:** Decide which activities and attractions are most important to you and allocate your budget accordingly. Consider purchasing tickets for popular attractions in advance to avoid queues and potentially benefit from pre-booking discounts.

Transportation:

- **Walking and cycling:** Montreux is a walkable and bike-friendly city. Consider walking or cycling to explore the city center and surrounding areas, saving on transportation costs and enjoying the scenery at the same time.
- **Public transport:** The efficient public transport system in Montreux offers a convenient and affordable way to get around. Purchase multi-day passes or travel cards for extended stays or frequent travel.
- **Taxis:** While generally safe, taxis can be expensive. Use taxis only for short distances or when necessary and agree on the fare before entering the vehicle.

Currency and Currency Exchange:

- **Switzerland uses the Swiss Franc (CHF):** Familiarize yourself with the current exchange rate between your home currency and CHF to budget effectively.
- **Consider using a travel credit card:** Many travel credit cards offer benefits like travel insurance, reward points, and favorable exchange rates, potentially saving you money compared to exchanging cash.
- **Beware of ATM fees:** When withdrawing cash from ATMs, be aware of potential withdrawal fees charged by your bank and the ATM operator.

Additional Tips:

- **Set a daily spending limit:** Set a realistic daily spending limit for yourself and track your expenses throughout your trip to avoid overspending.
- **Take advantage of free Wi-Fi:** Many restaurants, cafes, and public spaces in Montreux offer free Wi-Fi, allowing you to research and compare prices on attractions and restaurants, potentially saving money on data roaming charges.
- **Bargaining:** While not as common as in some other countries, light bargaining can sometimes be possible at flea markets or local shops.

By planning your budget in advance, understanding the cost considerations, and utilizing these tips, you can ensure a financially comfortable and enjoyable trip to the charming city of Montreux.

Local Customs and Etiquette

Greetings and Interactions:

- **Handshake is common:** A firm handshake with eye contact is the usual greeting when meeting someone for the first time.
- **Formal vs. informal:** In formal settings or when addressing someone for the first time, use titles like "Mr.," "Ms.," or "Madame" followed by the last name. In informal situations or with younger people, a simple "hello" or "bonjour" (French for hello) is sufficient.
- **Punctuality:** While not as strict as some cultures, punctuality is still valued in Montreux. Aim to be on time or slightly early for appointments and meetings.

Dining Etiquette:

- **Table manners:** Follow basic table manners, such as waiting for everyone to be served before beginning to eat and using utensils appropriately.
- **Tipping:** Tipping is not obligatory in Switzerland, but you can leave a small round-up to the nearest franc or a few francs as a sign of appreciation for good service.
- **Pace yourself:** Meals in Montreux tend to be multi-course affairs, so pace yourself and enjoy the experience.

Public Spaces and Transportation:

- **Respect personal space:** Maintain a comfortable distance from others, especially in crowded areas, and avoid speaking too loudly in public.
- **Give up your seat:** On public transport, offer your seat to the elderly, pregnant women, or passengers with disabilities.
- **Be mindful of noise:** Avoid loud noises or disruptive behavior in public spaces, such as libraries, museums, or restaurants.

Additional Tips:

- **Dress modestly:** While Montreux is a relaxed city, dress modestly when visiting religious sites or attending formal events.
- **Learn basic French phrases:** Learning a few basic French phrases like "hello," "thank you," and "excuse me" shows respect and can be helpful in navigating the city.
- **Respect the environment:** Switzerland takes pride in its environment. Dispose of waste responsibly and be mindful of your surroundings when exploring natural areas.

Understanding these customs and practicing basic etiquette will ensure you have a respectful and enriching experience while exploring the vibrant city of Montreux.

Sustainable Travel Practices

As you embark on your journey to Montreux, keep in mind the importance of responsible tourism. By adopting sustainable practices, you can minimize your environmental impact and contribute to the preservation of this beautiful destination for generations to come.

Transportation:

- **Public transportation champion:** Montreux boasts an excellent public transport system, including trains, buses, and boats. Opting for these options instead of private vehicles reduces your carbon footprint and allows you to experience the local way of life.
- **Explore by foot or bike:** The compact city center and surrounding areas are perfect for exploring on foot or by bike. This not only reduces your carbon footprint but also allows you to truly immerse yourself in the sights and sounds of the city.

- **Choose eco-friendly transportation:** If you must use a car, consider carpooling, renting an electric vehicle, or choosing a company that offers carbon offset options.

Accommodation:

- **Seek eco-certified hotels:** Look for hotels and other accommodations that have received eco-certifications. These establishments demonstrate a commitment to environmental sustainability through practices like energy and water conservation, waste reduction, and responsible sourcing.
- **Minimize water and energy use:** When staying in hotels or apartments, be mindful of your water and energy use. Take shorter showers, turn off lights and electronics when not in use, and consider opting for towel and linen reuse programs offered by some accommodations.

Food and Consumption:

- **Support local markets and restaurants:** Choosing locally sourced ingredients and supporting local businesses not only reduces your carbon footprint, but also ensures the freshest and most authentic culinary experience.
- **Reduce single-use plastics:** Bring your own reusable water bottle, shopping bags, and coffee cup to minimize single-use plastic waste.
- **Be mindful of food waste:** Order portions you can finish and avoid unnecessary food waste. Ask about composting options at restaurants if available.

Activities and Attractions:

- **Choose responsible tour operators:** When booking tours or activities, choose companies with a commitment to sustainable practices. Look for operators who minimize their environmental impact by using eco-friendly transportation, supporting local communities, and promoting responsible behavior in natural areas.

- **Respect the environment:** When exploring natural areas, adhere to designated trails, avoid disturbing wildlife, and pack out all your trash.
- **Embrace local culture:** Immerse yourself in the local culture by visiting museums, attending cultural events, and supporting local artisans. This not only enriches your experience but also contributes to the local economy and cultural preservation.

By making conscious choices and embracing these simple practices, you can contribute to a more sustainable future for Montreux and enjoy a truly responsible and rewarding trip.

Conclusion and Additional Resources

Useful Websites and Apps

As you plan your trip to Montreux, staying informed and having the right resources at your fingertips can be crucial for a smooth and enjoyable experience. Here are some helpful websites and apps to consider:

Official Websites:

- **Montreux Riviera Tourism:** https://www.montreuxriviera.com/en/ - This website is your one-stop shop for everything related to Montreux and the surrounding region, offering information on attractions, events, accommodation, transport, and more.
- **Switzerland Tourism:** https://www.myswitzerland.com/en/ - This official website of Switzerland Tourism provides comprehensive

information on the entire country, including Montreux. Find details on travel planning, cultural experiences, and regional specialties.
- **Swiss Federal Railways (SBB):** https://www.sbb.ch/en - Plan your train journeys throughout Switzerland with the SBB website or app.
- **Compagnie Générale de Navigation (CGN):** https://www.cgn.ch/en/ - This website allows you to explore the Montreux Riviera Cruise options and purchase tickets.

Useful Apps:

- **Montreux Riviera App:** This app offers a comprehensive guide to the region, including offline maps, event listings, travel recommendations, and public transportation information.
- **SBB Mobile App:** The SBB Mobile App allows you to purchase train tickets, access real-time travel information, and plan your journey on the go.
- **Google Translate:** This app can come in handy for translating menus, signs, and basic communication during your trip.
- **TripIt:** This app helps you organize your travel itinerary, store travel documents, and receive real-time travel alerts.
- **Moovit:** This app provides real-time public transportation information, including bus and tram schedules, routes, and directions, helping you navigate the city efficiently.

Additional Resources:

- **Google Maps:** Utilize Google Maps for navigation, finding points of interest, and exploring the city.
- **Instagram:** Follow the official Instagram accounts of Montreux Riviera Tourism (@montreuxriviera) and local businesses to get inspiration for your trip and discover hidden gems.

By utilizing these websites and apps, you can:

- **Plan your itinerary effectively.**
- **Access real-time information about transportation and attractions.**
- **Communicate and navigate with ease.**
- **Discover hidden gems and unique experiences.**

Remember, staying connected and informed throughout your trip will ensure you get the most out of your visit to the captivating city of Montreux.

Acknowledgment

I hope this travel guide equips you for a smooth, enjoyable, and enriching experience in this captivating Swiss city. Remember, from exploring the charming towns and breathtaking scenery to indulging in delicious local cuisine and engaging in responsible travel practices, Montreux has something to offer everyone.

So, pack your bags, embrace the adventure, and create lasting memories in the heart of the Swiss Riviera!

Bon voyage!

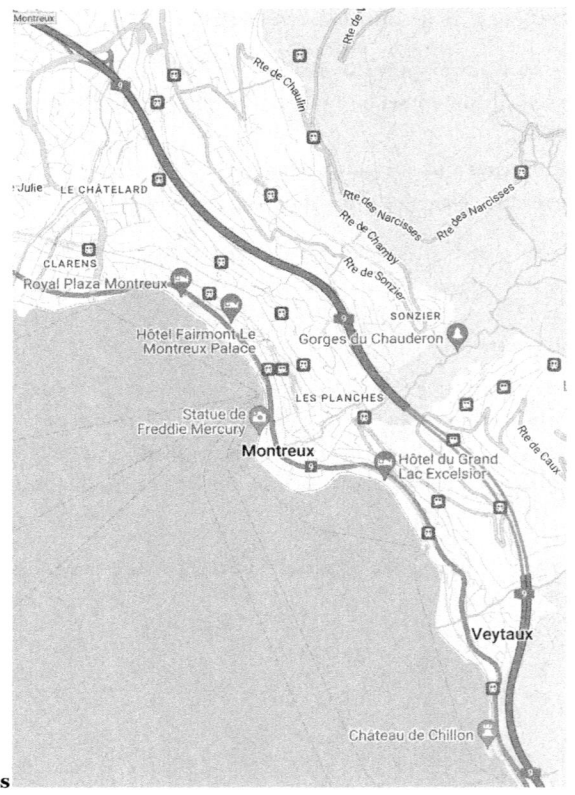

Maps

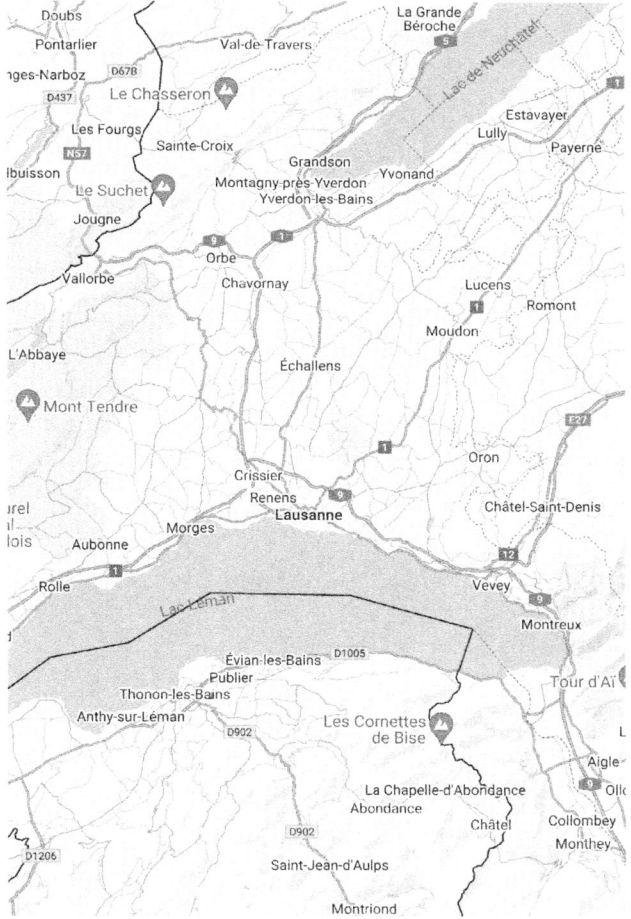

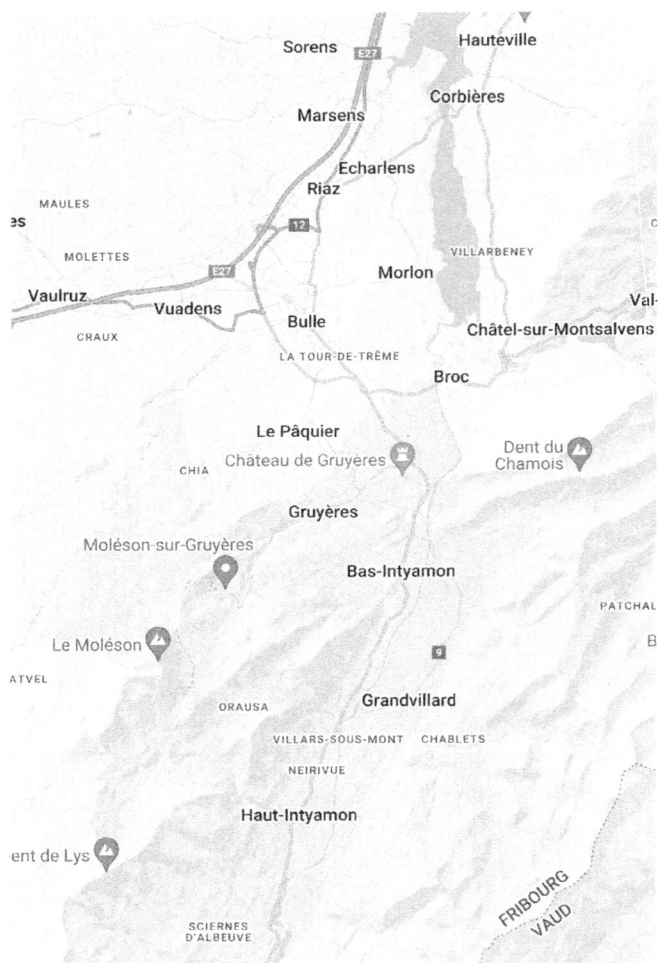

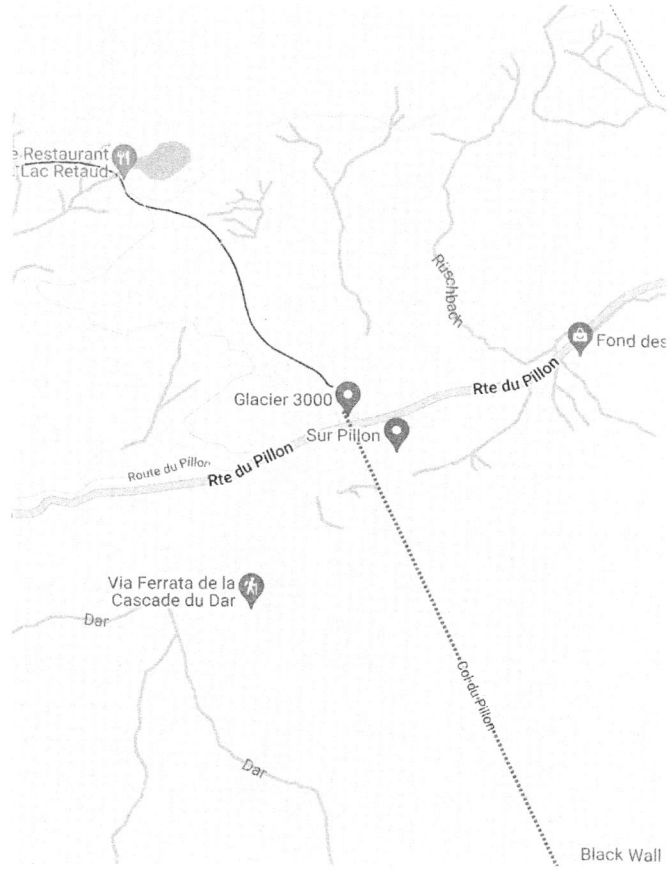

Printed in Great Britain
by Amazon